GETTING THE BEST FROM YOUR AD AGENCY

Everything Marketers Need to Know about Working with Agencies — From Creative, Media Planning, Budgeting and Market Strategy to Campaign Execution and Evaluation.

JOE MARCONI

PROBUS PUBLISHING COMPANY
Chicago, Illinois

This publication is designed to provide accurate and authoritative information in regard to the subject matter covered. It is sold with the understanding that the publisher is not engaged in rendering legal, accounting or other professional service. If legal advice or other expert assistance is required, the services of a competent professional person should be sought.

Library of Congress Cataloging in Publication Data Available

ISBN 1-55738-179-8

Printed in the United States of America

   BC

1 2 3 4 5 6 7 8 9 0

*To Glory, without whose patience
and understanding this book would not
have been possible.*

Contents

Preface

This is a book for people in advertising who have to work with other people in advertising—and want to do it better. Advertising is a fascinating and multi-disciplined process. Creative and business people come together brimming with ideas and plans and often clash head on. We will try to keep this from happening since careers, billions of dollars and the future of a business or product may depend on it.

This book is not a course in interpersonal relationships. If, however, you've ever taken such a course you are well ahead, for the core of our subject is working together. This is also not a course in advertising. If your objective is getting the best and the most from your advertising agency, we must begin with certain assumptions:

1   That you are the person (or one of the persons) responsible for your business or company's advertising;

2   That you have (or are about to select) an advertising agency;

3   And (this is the big one) that you are a *believer*—
someone who accepts the principle that the right message
targeted to the right audience through the right media
with sufficient frequency can produce tremendous results.

We've looked at some campaigns that have worked
and some that haven't. We have examined fundamental
elements of successful working relationships and repeat-
edly asked at varying intervals is this worth the cost in
money or energy?

Whether your role is that of agency chief, client, or
consultant, the collective result should provide you with
a strategic outline for *Getting the Best from your Ad Agency*.

I would like to thank Richard W. Ronvik, Terry and
David Bogdan, Joe Cappo, Ron Cohn, and Ron Millman
for support, encouragement and assistance in completing
this project. Special thanks as well to Michael Jeffers,
Pamela van Giessen and Michael Ryder, my new friends
at Probus Publishing.

Overview

Advertising professionals, whether with an agency or as clients, are used to hearing what's wrong with advertising...

"There's too much of it—too many commercials and they're too loud . . . too much clutter in magazines and much too much in the Sunday newspapers especially. . . Do they really think anybody reads all that? . . . Advertising insults my intelligence. It makes all those outrageous claims and the stuff never looks or works as well as it does in the ads. . . It presents a bad example for kids. . ."

When it comes to advertising, everyone has an opinion. By 1990, with some $30 billion annually spent on American television advertising alone and more than $110 billion total, that's a lot of opinions. Add print, outdoor, radio, direct mail, sales promotions, and telemarketing and you have an industry with more money and influence than many entire countries can claim.

When a consumer (or for that matter, an advertiser) looks at an ad, rejects it, and says "I may not be an expert, but I know what I like," he or she has offered a very valid critique. When an advertiser or agency says "You're missing the point of the ad," then the ad has failed. Good advertising, plainly put, makes its point and should never have to be explained.

1

There are many definitions of advertising, some so rambling and convoluted as to make you forget why you even asked. One simple definition says advertising is using purchased time or space to present your message.

What? Nothing about selling? After all, isn't the whole point of advertising to sell?

Not entirely. Stores sell and salespeople sell. A coupon in an ad may be for selling. Basically, the function of advertising is to create awareness and recognition and provide information about a product or service—to create a desire for it. Closing the sale isn't the ad's responsibility.

These pages present some points that may sometimes seem pretty basic. The tremendous success of Robert Fulghum's 1989 bestseller, *All I Really Needed to Know I Learned in Kindergarten*, should tell us something just in its title. A lot of what we know about working well with others we learned when we were very young—in preschool, on the playground, on the football or swimming team, in the band, learning to dance . . . pick your own time or place in your memory. The essence of working well with others—using patience, understanding, respect, appreciation, and good humor—is something we are taught at a young age, but we often seem to need to be reminded in order to keep our personal and professional course on track.

Building on these solid, old-fashioned principles we will look at your company's size, shape, and needs and match them to what an ad agency has to offer. We'll look at whether a consultant would be an asset to the process, saving time, money, and providing expertise, or merely an expensive burden. We will review some of the resources you may not have realized were available to you.

Many people have described the agency/client relationship as a partnership, even a marriage. Like a marriage it is definitely a close working relationship involving mutual interests and respect, and it should be positive and satisfying. Both sides should be committed to working toward its success. Reasonable allowances and understanding should be provided. But it is also a *business*—to both parties. When egos and disenchantment surface, and conflicting goals arise, it may be time to consider a marriage counsellor, or even a divorce.

We look very closely at the strengths of the relationship in light of varying functions, and create a framework that avoids duplicating efforts. We also cut through the wall of alphabet blocks that often keeps us from understanding each other (CPMs, GRPs, ADIs, and so on).

Once we've settled on *who* will do *what*, we'll look at how we approach the assignment. With humor? Case histories? Testimonials? Movie stars? Beethoven or rock & roll? We'll look at some notable successes and failures.

As with anything else, the ad business *is* a business, with all of the demands, pressures and competitive rivalries to match the most high-powered law firm, Wall Street brokerage, or airline job.

In a good ad agency/client relationship, everybody wins. The creative staff and the account service people are rewarded for excellent performance. The client gets more business and greater recognition. Everyone makes money. Obviously, the opposite is true of the relationship where it doesn't all come together. It's easy to see how inflated egos can bring on disaster, but usually it is more subtle. Simple miscues can result in production cost overruns, missed media opportunities, and wasted time and energy in the strategic and creative stages. Then nobody wins. Everybody looks stupid. Bad blood rises and mistrust or lack of confidence produces a strained, crippled working relationship. Our challenge is to keep this from happening; our jobs depend on it.

Everyone has his or her role in the process. The client team might include any number of vice presidents, directors, managers, and people without titles, but with very important roles. The agency team may have an account supervisor, account executive, creative director, art directors, copy writers, and any number of production assistants. Many of these individuals will have overlapping responsibilities. Most believe themselves to be creative, competent professionals. If history holds true, they won't always agree on the best tactics to employ, let alone the best strategy. What began being compared to a marriage may end being compared to a war or at least an adversarial relationship.

Our ultimate goal is to achieve a just and lasting peace between client and agency. We will, however, settle for merely making very good advertising.

Advertising has had its share of stereotypes: *The Hucksters; The Man in the Gray Flannel Suit; The Image Makers;* the bumbling "Darren" on TV's *Bewitched;* and the angst-riddled, obsessively trendy Michael and Elliott of TV's *thirtysomething;* professional, pipe-smoking, distinguished elder statesman, David Ogilvy; the enigmatic brothers Saatchi and Saatchi; wildly irreverent Jerry Della Femina; and the intimidating, tough Roger Ailes. Advertising has given the world geniuses as well as people who should be ashamed of themselves. This volume aims to contribute to a greater appreciation of and understanding among advertising professionals.

Finding the Right Agency

The Right Ad Agency for Your Company

This first section does not include the words "choosing" in its title because, before setting about selecting, we should first determine *absolutely* that there is a need to look. Let's assume that an agency/client relationship exists. Why change it? Some of the most common reasons are:

- A new ad director joins the company or is promoted to the position and wants to make a fresh start with a whole new team.

- The company has become dissatisfied with the agency for any number of reasons, from unacceptable creative, inadequate service, and questionable billings to frequent account personnel changes.

- The company and agency disagree over strategy—how to approach the advertising challenge.

- One outgrows the other. Either the account becomes too large for the agency (or too small and reduces its budget and requirements to where it can

5

r afford the agency) or the agency grows, ᵖₗₐₛ ᵤₚ some sizeable business, and can no longer afford to handle clients of comparatively small size.

- Conflicts. The agency has acquired a new client who poses a conflict or it merges, acquires, or is acquired by another agency which represents a conflicting client.

- Money. Clearly one of the most unpleasant reasons to change agencies has to do with the issue of compensation; the client feels it is being overcharged or is simply not getting its money's worth.

Any one of these reasons is just grounds for ending a relationship. However, any of them can be negotiated if both parties really want to stay together. Losing an account is, in most cases, both costly and demoralizing to an agency. Of course agencies sometimes resign accounts for reasons just as legitimate as those that prompt the client to make the move. Some clients are just absolutely horrible to work with. The Gallo Wine and Helmsley Hotels accounts are two notorious examples, both known for heaping abuse on agency personnel according to trade press accounts.

But the majority of cases find the client deciding to change its agency, and as our main focus in this work is *getting the best and the most from your ad agency*, let's consider these points:

Changing ad agencies is costly. You have an investment in professional time and education. Your people have spent a lot of time with their people. Changing ad agencies means taking time to prepare a list, weed-out, interview and evaluate other agencies then give them a grace or learning period to get up-to-speed on your company or industry. This is all time you could be devoting to generating first-class advertising.

Having summarized reasons to part company (and of course there could be others), let's look a bit closer at some of them from a professional perspective. Is a split *truly* in the company's best interests from a cost or efficiency standpoint?

In a situation involving a new ad director, consider the legitimacy of changing agencies so that the new director can put together his or her own team. Perhaps this is something that was one of the conditions of the job, a promise or demand. It seems reasonable that whoever comes in with a mandate to shake things up or change direction or otherwise make a difference should be allowed the opportunity to do so.

Robert Townsend offers advice for success in his landmark 1970 bestseller, *Up the Organization*. Chapter One, page one offers the lines, "Fire the whole advertising department and your old agency. Then go get the best new agency you can."

There's a lot to be said for getting a fresh start, cleaning the slate, starting with a blank page.

There's also an expression that states "if it ain't broke, don't fix it."

The new ad director may be taking over for a variety of reasons—a successor who quit or died, a merger, perhaps. Because a new person is in charge doesn't inherently mean everything else is wrong.

Mr. Townsend, an extremely bright, funny, and successful man, likes to practice what he calls corporate "guerrilla warfare," shaking things up, getting the juices flowing. This approach is terrific . . . when it is the approach needed.

Too often a new person puts too great an emphasis on cosmetic changes. Move around the furniture; rearrange the pictures on the wall. It's fine for directors to feel they need to put their own stamp on things, but change costs money and an executive in charge of something as creative as advertising should be sensitive to what changes are made and what those changes cost the company.

Fire the ad agency if they aren't getting the job done, not just for the sake of change.

Consider the new chairman of a marketing committee which oversaw advertising for a large financial operation. He was not an advertising man, but a professional investor. Summoning his ad agency people to his office the week he took over, he said simply and directly, "My philosophy is to change lawyers, accountants, and ad agencies every two years. It keeps them fresh and hungry. You've had this account for four years now. Don't take it personally, it's just the way I work. You're fired."

He was certainly within his rights to do that. Furthermore, he was right. People fresh to an assignment *do generally* bring a whole new exciting sense of that freshness to the project. Nevertheless, his decision was, quite simply, stupid. His was a business that required considerable knowledge before a new agency could produce really good work. That knowledge would take six months to a year for the new agency to acquire. The agency he fired had also been producing award-winning, effective work on a budget half the size of the competition's. They deserved a chance to retain business they had worked hard to learn and earn. The decision was arrogant and unprofessional. Two years later, the succeeding agency, having done fairly unspectacular work, didn't have to worry. The change-oriented executive had moved on to other responsibilities and had been replaced by someone who didn't much care to make changes as long as the business was profitable. It was and he didn't. The net result was that a good agency lost a large account and an advertiser lost a good agency and team, to say nothing of the individuals involved, people who took their jobs seriously, did them well, and deserved better.

Evaluating The Existing Agency Relationship

When a new ad director takes over, there is a fairly simple system that helps focus attention on the task at hand. It is pretty much the same procedure any manager might follow:

1 *Prepare a situation analysis.* Where are you in your industry and relative to your competition? What are the major problems you must consider or overcome? What history can you draw upon?

2 *Define your objective.* Be realistic and be specific, whether the goal is better name recognition or more sales. Quantify your goals. Set a specific percentage increase you're looking for in awareness, sales, number of markets, and so on.

3 *Allocate responsibility for achieving your objectives.* Define precisely the responsibilities of both your advertising department and your advertising agency.

Evaluate your agency according to these criteria:

- Do they understand your objectives?
- Are they responsive and service oriented?
- Are they creative?
- Is their work for you getting results?
- Are they absolutely giving you the best value for your ad budget?
- Does the agency *listen* at meetings and respond with solutions?
- Does the finished work conform to or exceed the directives?
- Are projects completed on schedule?
- Are they within budget or quoted estimates?

Decide whether the problems are real or perceived and whether or not it is the agency's fault. Hold your agency accountable to deliver for you, but don't make them the scapegoat for problems elsewhere in the relationship. Firing the agency won't likely make those problems disappear.

If the answer to any of these questions is no, a meeting is in order. (This, of course, should hold true whether the ad director is new to the job or a fixture at the company.) Determine the reason for failure to meet the criteria. Perhaps the agency received vague or conflicting directives, or was working "to order" (following specific creative directives, as opposed to being allowed a free creative hand). Should you determine a miscommunication has occurred and the agency may not be totally to blame, give them another chance to show what they can do. It's cheaper in the long run than going through a search and review process for a new agency.

This brings us to the second of our reasons why advertisers change agencies: a general or specific dissatisfaction with the relationship. Perhaps a most critical element for success is chemistry. Once you've established credentials and skills, knowledge and experience, the agency/client relationship still cannot work if the chemistry isn't right. That doesn't mean you have to become best friends or tennis partners, but it does mean that you have to *feel good* about working together. Even in relationships where people don't *like* each other, a level of professional respect, courtesy, maturity, and competence can carry the relationship to success. If the teaming just doesn't feel like it's going to work, chances are it won't.

Another reason for change stems from the larger issue of dissatisfaction, but it deserves consideration on its own. How far is either side willing to go to compromise when there isn't a clear agreement as to either the strategy or the approach to the problem? When an agency gets so locked into an idea the client doesn't like that something's got to give, that something is often the relationship. Clients often tell agencies what headline, copy, photo, typeface, illustration, and model must be used along with the logo (conforming, of course, to the corporate identity usage manual), and where the ad can run. Otherwise, the agency is free to be as creative as it wishes. This reduces the agency to little more than a go-between for the client and media, and a high-priced one at that. If the agency really needs the income and doesn't have strong objections to the quality of the material provided, they are likely to go along with this arrangement—but uneasily. The agency and client both realize that the agency is not doing what advertising agencies are supposed to do: create and produce good advertising on demand or as part of a team. In the example given above, the agency is an order-taker. In other cases ad agencies have been known to have "trunk ideas," a collection of generic creative work in search of a client or product. Some agencies should (and do) resign accounts when they believe they are asked to compromise their creative integrity. Some clients should (and do) fire agencies for not listening or reacting badly to what the job requires.

The reasons for change that derive from one side outgrowing the other or the acquisition of conflicting accounts really don't need elaboration. But, the issue of compensation is another matter. Among the most painful phrases an agency can hear is "I've got a problem with your bill." Obviously errors occur, both human and technical. When a bill for services seems excessive or not in conformance with estimates, clients will be concerned with more than billing procedures. They may well question the honesty or integrity of the agency itself. If it happens more than once, they will probably start looking at other agencies, and rightly so. Questions are fine as a matter of clarifying a description of services for the accounting department, but a good agency will never leave its client an opportunity to doubt its integrity.

If you are satisfied that for reasons of chemistry, cost, creativity, or service, the right course is a new ad agency, the process need not be a painful one. Some companies approach the search and selection stage with committees and forms and multi-page questionnaires. Others find short cuts to save time, money and frustration. The most frustrating occurrence of all is to go through the process and find that the newly selected agency is no improvement over the old one for a new set of reasons. Or, as an old TV commercial for Alka-Seltzer used to claim, "like trading a headache for an upset stomach."

There are no guarantees, but in terms of where to look, how to look and what to look for, there are some guidelines to follow, which are described in the next section.

Getting Started: How and Where to Begin Looking for an Ad Agency

What qualities are most important to you in choosing your advertising agency? This being a matter of opinion, there are likely to be as many opinions as the number of people asked.

The first step in identifying your prospective agency is to designate the person or persons within your organization who will constitute your "search committee." Ideally this should consist of no more than three people with an understanding of the advertising function. The advertising director (or marketing director) should chair this committee.

With your search committee created, look closely at your own company. Before inviting agencies to submit proposals for your business you should have a succinct sense of what that business represents. Answer these questions:

1   Is this account "corporate," for a product, service, institution . . . or other?

2   To whom will the agency be accountable as as client contact and will that person have direct decision-making authority for the ad program?

3   What's your *real* ad budget? Look at what you have budgeted for several years and compare that figure to

what you actually spent. If there is a variance, try to determine why. Did the agency go over budget? Did you budget more than you spent because the business climate changed and you cut back?

4   What will be the range of services you will require from the agency?
Research?
Media buying?
Sales promotion?
Public relations?
Strategic planning?
Other?

How to Get the Best (and the Most) from Your Ad Agency

These pages offer guidelines with the objective of creating a framework within which terrific advertising can grow. Good advertising that succeeds starts with the "seeds." Maybe it is a new creative idea or maybe it's a slogan or theme line that's been around for generations. Maybe it's something as unexpected as someone in your organization committing to sponsorship of a charity event or agreeing to be the sole advertiser on a cluster of airport billboards—and that commitment places *you* at the center of the campaign. Whatever the origin, motivation or idea, some process has been set in motion and an evolution must occur.

We can analyze the structure and components of good advertising or we can just get on with it. Often, art directors will say they need to see copy first to know how much space they'll have in which to work. Copywriters will have to know time and space parameters (a thirty-second radio spot, fifteen-second TV spot, quarter page of newspaper, magazine spread . . .). The media buyer won't give the time and space specs until the budget's in—why go through the efforts of costing-out spreads in

The New Yorker when the client will likely only agree to one-third pages in trade magazines?

The creative director's position is, "Will the client expect an idea with a new visual, fresh theme line and totally innovative approach . . . or a new spin on what's perceived as what the audience for the product has come to expect?"

Create an environment that helps the advertiser sell the product. After that everything else is negotiable. Research will sometimes be commissioned and ignored. Creative ideas will be developed and scrapped. Commercials will be produced and never run, media will be bought and canceled.

Sometimes any of these occurrences are worth the expense. On the surface these may seem like a master plan of indecision, even incompetence, and the worst examples of egos out of control.

Maybe not. Let's say, for example, you've tested a theme line that says "there was never a better time to invest," and use a leading business analyst and author as the celebrity presenter of your line in a television commercial during a major Sunday sports event.

It looks good—except the preceding Friday, the stock market drops 200 points (it happened twice in the 1980s, proving both volatility and that the stock market hates Fridays), making your well-tested campaign line an embarrassment.

And then your celebrity suffers a heart attack and is rushed to the hospital, an event also noted on the evening news.

This story comes on right after the one about violent winds and storm . . . which caused the cancellation of Sunday's major sports event.

Unlikely? Silly? Not if you were a sponsor of the World Series games canceled after the 1989 San Francisco earthquake or the major televised events canceled that same year due to last-minute intensive coverage of a hur-

ricane ravaging the southern United States and nearby islands.

Yes, the best, most carefully tested plans can go
awry. Good planning always includes a contingency or
fallback plan. The focus here, however, will be largely on
those kinder, gentler times when the stock market doesn't
crash, the earth doesn't quake, hurricanes only concentrate their fury on distant, uninhabited islands, and people want to buy what we have to sell if we all do our job
right.

We will outline our guidelines and then elaborate on
them in such a way as to establish their legitimacy. Much
of this material should be rather non-controversial; the
"golden rule" never stirs much debate, and persons responsible for managing an advertising program generally
possess the native intelligence to know that *when you treat
people well, they perform well.*

True, some believe that it is *payment,* not *treatment*
that should guide the quality of performance. While compensation is a *component* of the process, it is not the process in and of itself.

Consider the following relevant aphorisms:

- The secret of education lies in respect for the stu-
  dent.
- There are those who listen—and those who simply
  wait to talk.
- Lead, follow, or get out of the way.

These three statements are simple, direct and all propose cooperation, respect, and understanding as guidelines to success. Here are some others more pertinent to
advertising and phrased perhaps less eloquently, but
more specifically to the point:

1 *Believe in advertising.* If advertising is only a line item
on the budget and you are not convinced of its value,
don't do it, or at least put its management in the hands of

someone who does recognize its worth. Simply stated, just as an employee who only "puts in time" rarely gets the same results or satisfaction as one who enjoys and believes in the job, an ad campaign guided by someone who does not accept or recognize the power and value of good advertising will likely falter, or at best achieve mediocre results. Terms like "pilot" program often mean that you don't have enough confidence in your plan to give it 100 percent. If you don't believe in it, don't do it.

2 *Believe in your advertising.* Be excited about what you're doing or refine and improve it until you are. Your enthusiasm and encouragement should set the tone for others on your team. If you don't think you've got a terrific idea, it is unlikely your colleagues will feel motivated to push the campaign.

3 *Know what you want.* Every ad program or marketing plan must have a clear objective. Use research. Brainstorm. Test. It is often *said* that the work or the agency failed to meet the client's expectations. It is often *true* that the client failed to make clear those expectations . . . or sometimes even to know what they were. We often hear the phrase, "They don't know what they want, so how can we give it to them?" There is, frankly, no excuse for this. Professionals should be smart enough to not commit time and money to a plan that is not carefully defined.

4 *Have a plan.* Whether the client writes it or the agency writes it, whether it is called the marketing plan, strategic plan, game plan, or strategy outline, *focus.* Going into the marketplace without the basic plan framework (objectives, strategy and tactics, budget) is stupid, costly, and doomed to failure.

5 *Know when to talk.* Lead or at least participate in the development of the situation analysis, establishing objectives and setting the budget. Be clear about your sense of what needs to be done.

6 *Know when to listen.* Often a person will develop a narrow view, based on company politics, personal preferences, habit, or insulation from outside appraisals. You've hired an agency; don't turn them into high-priced order-takers. Listen to *their* analysis of your market or competitive situation and consider their case objectively. The goal is to develop and run a successful campaign, not to pay someone to tell you what they think you want to hear.

7   *Show respect.* Many companies and firms think of or refer to their ad agencies as "vendors." This is demeaning and shows a lack of respect as well as a lack of understanding of what an agency can and should represent.

8   *Commit yourself to your plan.* Remember the expression, "Lead, follow, or get out of the way." Make your commitment to the success of your effort virtually a divine crusade. Whether you've written your plan or someone you've hired has written it, once you say go, really *go!*

9   *Don't waste your agency's time.* This advice seems like simple good business practice, yet often there will be "just one more thing" that generates a phone call that really doesn't need to be made on a subject that often has nothing to do with the ad program. Many clients believe that if an agency works on a commission basis and service is factored into that commission, it doesn't matter how frequent or lengthy phone calls or meetings are; they believe it's all part of getting their money's worth. Some clients use their agencies to arbitrate disputes between departments or even run errands. An agency will rarely decline such a request from a client, but ask yourself if you would have *your* lawyer take time to do such chores. If you treat your agency with a high level of professionalism, you'll find projects are completed faster and at less cost.

10   *Be specific.* When communicating with the agency, tell them what you want. As stated in the third item, an agency will most assuredly fall short of your expectations if they don't *know* your expectations. Certainly, that also means to make clear what you *don't* want.

11 *Cooperate.* This sounds easier than it is, especially when a lot of important individuals gather around one table. Remember, though, that you have a real (or assumed) particular expertise in your industry—one that your agency can't be assumed to have. *They,* of course, have done their homework and presumably have skills you don't have (which is why you hired them). Your staffwriter, speechwriter, or PR person should not be writing ad copy. In short: work together, not in competition.

12 *Compromise.* This is not the same as cooperate. Keep in mind this quote: "I have *my* way; you have *your* way; there is no *the* way."

13 *Be open to change, willing to experiment or stretch.* To fall back on the old argument, "Because that's how we've always done it," is no justification for not testing what may prove to be a great idea.

14 *Know your market.* Don't make assumptions about your market. If you don't know your market, buy research on it. Knowing who makes up your market, what they do and don't like forms the cornerstone of your campaign, from packaging to creative theme to media selection. Clients often claim that their product is "perfect for the market." But is it, or is that remark wishful thinking? Research is held in high esteem by many clients, and rightly so. Is there a market for your product? At what cost? In what regions, or at what times of the year? Men or women? Young, old, or both? How do color and music affect your sales? If you have research, give it to your agency. If you don't have research, demand that your agency undertake its development. Knowing your market is ultimately beneficial to every aspect of your business. Sometimes research will be expensive and only confirm what is already known. It's still worth it—especially when it tells us that what we thought was right is wrong.

15 *Know your costs.* At nearly every level, cost awareness is a characteristic of competence and professionalism.

Some clients will request such promotions as running a commercial during the Super Bowl or buying a full-page in *The Wall Street Journal* without the slightest idea of the cost. Have at least a general idea of the cost for the use of a radio announcer's voice, or the exclusive usage fee for a stock photograph or talent and residual payments. Even the cost of duplicating tapes can run into big dollars. These "agency costs" ultimately are "client costs." If you are retaining an agency on a fee basis, be sure your employees know that when they phone or ask for a meeting with agency staff, the meter is running.

16 *Resist trends.* Use research, but rely on your own experience and the experience and skill of those you've hired. For example, giving up a successful media formula because the trade press says everyone is turning to direct mail or sales promotion or telemarketing or using celebrities is senseless. TV works. Newspapers work. Magazines, mail, and outdoor advertising work. Dare to be different . . . *and dare to stay the same* if you know that what's being done works. Being creative doesn't mean changing to emulate someone else. Good ideas are waiting to happen, but don't pull the plug on a successful campaign before it's time.

17 *React—get excited.* If you don't like the agency's work, say so. They should be prepared for such a response, and either have alternatives or a strong case for why their presentation will succeed. If you like what you see, let them know that too. Work that doesn't excite a client probably won't impress readers, viewers or other audiences for the ad.

18 *Send and request meeting reports.* Even professional communicators often miscommunicate with each other. If you have an internal meeting that affects the ad program (for instance a budget review or analysis of ad responses) notify the agency. Too often, clients assume agency people are aware of changes or decisions which are made at client meetings but never communicated. A summary of agency/client meetings doesn't have to be long or de-tailed but can—and nearly always does—avoid misun-derstandings about how much is being allocated for what by when. It's unfortunate but true that people listen selec-tively and often hear things differently. Write it down.

19 *Relax and let your agency do what you hired them to do.* Enjoy this process. Although it's been said many times, many ways, this is at the core of much of the tension that develops between clients and their ad agencies. Of course the company has bright, competent professionals who un-derstand a thing or two about effective communication, and of course people like to show off or are insecure. Nevertheless, you have talked to many people at many agencies and have selected the agency you did because they looked like they could do the job for you. Tell them what you want and how much you have allocated for it, then back off and let them work. If they don't get the job done, give them another chance or replace them. Don't get frustrated about how you "had to write the copy" yourself. *Require* the agency to do it. The client who so totally runs its advertising program—writing copy, writ-ing headlines, reworking the art director's or creative director's submissions—is not only insulting and demean-ing the agency, but wasting their own money and re-sources. A good ad agency team may be disappointed or frustrated at hearing that a client doesn't like the work and wants to see something else, but professionally speaking, it is a more correct response than a client re-doing or altering work submitted. This does not mean agency and client shouldn't talk to each other and work together as a team, but it again emphasizes the same level of respect accorded other professionals, such as a lawyer or accountant, whose work a client would not presume to change. A good agency will solicit client input *before* cre-ating advertising. It is said that when it comes to adver-tising, everyone's an expert. Don't confuse opinion with expertise. Get what you pay for. Let the agency do the job you hired them to do.

20 *Pay your bills.* Advertising is very expensive. Many clients will have hundreds of thousands of dollars in creative, production, and media expenses outstanding for months. This creates strains on even the largest agencies. Know your costs and pay your bills fairly and promptly.

20 Guidelines in Review
[How many have you forgotten already?]

1   Believe in advertising.

2   Believe in *your* advertising.

3   Know what you want.

4   Have a plan.

5   Know when to talk.

6   Know when to listen.

7   Show respect.

8   Commit to your plan.

9   Don't waste your agency's time.

10   Be specific.

11   Cooperate.

12   Compromise.

13   Be open to change.

14   Know your market.

15   Know what things cost.

16   Resist trends.

17   React—get excited.

18   Send and request meeting reports.

19   Let your agency do what you hired them to do.

20   Pay your bills.

Getting on with Your Search: Narrowing the Field

Create a profile of your ideal agency, listing the character-istics and qualities, in order of priority, you believe might distinguish one agency from another. As a starting point, answer these ten questions in a way that works best for you. Perhaps a simple *important/unimportant* response is sufficient. You may want to weight your responses from one to ten, with *one* being "relatively unimportant" and *ten* being "very important."

1   Is knowledge of (and experience with other clients in) your industry an important consideration?   _____
If yes, should the agency have worked on an account in your industry during the past year?   _____

2   How important is "creative" in your selection of an agency?   _____

3   Should the agency be regarded as specialists in any particular area or discipline such as television production, direct mail, sales promotion, print or telemarketing? (Circle one that may apply or note an area if not listed). _____

4   How important is the agency's having a research ca-pability?   _____
If important, must it be in-house?   _____

5   Should the agency have in-house media planners and buyers?   _____

6   How important is it that the agency have won awards for its work?   _____

7   How important a consideration is the age/experience level of the people assigned to work on your account?   _____

8   How important is the agency's size, in terms of
(a)   billings?   _____
(b)   number of offices?   _____
(c)   number of employees?   _____
(d)   number of other clients?   _____

9   How important is the agency's range of capabilities (such as public relations, event management, newsletters and other collateral and sales promotions?   _____

10   How important is the agency's willingness to negotiate a compensation arrangement (of a fee verses a standard commission arrangement)?   _____

From the answers to these questions you should be able to determine pretty much the type of agency with which you might have a solid and comfortable working relationship. Begin to list your important considerations in order of priority, first listing those to which you answered "very important" (or rated ten) or close to it in order of importance.

Consider carefully how strongly you really feel about your responses:

- *Do you really care if your agency used to work for a competitor?* Would that most likely be a plus or a minus? You might like to hear from your agency how your competition approached issues, but you also might like no more than a clear, concise analysis and response to an issue. At the time you saw examples of the work on behalf of your competition, were you impressed? Indifferent? Envious?

- *Do you really care if the agency's research operation is in-house or an outside contracted service?* One agency boasts the greatest number of PHD's and the largest computer outside of the Pentagon at the center of its research capability. Is that important to you or is it an excessive expense?

- *What about agency in-house media?* There are several points to consider. If you are dealing with a small-to medium-size agency with a single office, but you need a strong schedule of radio and outdoor advertising in five cities in a mix of major and secondary markets, you may want to subcontract or assign the media portion of your account to a media buying service. The standard reasoning is that a single location agency will have neither the knowledge nor the buying power necessary to make the best deals with radio stations in distant markets, while a media service purchasing quantities of time and space in many markets will have much more clout as well as expertise. This may or may not be the case. Some small-to-medium size agencies, represented by an intelligent person who really wants the business, using a computer, the latest *Standard Rate and Data* directories and a telephone, can do as fine a job of negotiating and buying as you can possibly get. The best approach is to make in-house media a point of discussion with your prospective agency. Find out how they approach their task and how much they know. Most good agencies know their limitations; they buy what they can and bring in a subcontractor (perhaps a media service or regional rep) to work with them. This is an example of how being *smart* is more important than *size*.

- *To some clients, awards are very important*—They symbolize a recognition of excellence or achievement. To others, of course, they are meaningless and self-serving. It is the *results* achieved by the work, not the recognition of its creativity, that is important. There is legitimacy to both sides of the debate. At all times the paramount consideration should be that *the work does what it is supposed to do*—whether that's to help increase sales or increase recognition and raise awareness of the advertiser's product or service. When work succeeds, a plaque or trophy is certainly in order. But like getting an *Oscar* for a film no one went to see, recognition for quality in an endeavor that fails to find an audience is hollow at best. In short, awards are nice, but ask about the agency's *quantifiable successes* before assigning them to your project.

- *Age and experience are always issues when considering people to work on your account.* To some clients it is important that the agency's principal or a partner be in charge of the account team. Some clients like "youth and energy" on the agency team and believe the expertise on the client side is enough of a factor; other clients want only a "seasoned pro" to work on the account. Some are turned off by gray hair and gray flannel suits. The bottom line is that *the competent agency professional* should get the nod, regardless of age or experience, because the real pro will bring in or consult with persons who will add other dimensions to the quality of the work. Solid professionals do whatever is required. A thirty-year-old account manager, new to an auto account, if a real pro, would bring in a consulting expert on automobile advertising. (Actually, this person wouldn't likely be the account manager of an auto client without *some* strength and knowledge of the product, but good advertising people do their homework, learn their clients' business and *still* call in the reserves as needed). The issue isn't youth or age, experience or inexperience; it's choosing a competent professional who truly wants your business and will do what's necessary to succeed.

- *When considering the size of an appropriate agency, some things are obvious.* A global company based in Los Angeles with a budget of $20 million shouldn't be talking to a two-partner agency in Cleveland with total billings of $3 million. Likewise, a company with an ad budget of $650,000 (a lot to *them*) is not of much interest to Leo Burnett. But the rules are changing as bigger agencies, in desperate need of more business, are taking on smaller and smaller clients and bigger companies are taking a chance on smaller agencies. The first rule is to be honest with yourself and realistic about what will be appropriate for your company. Check to see what some of the large companies are spending on advertising and compare those numbers to your own budget. If you are not spending close to the $2 billion spent by the Philip Morris Companies, don't feel like a piker. Even if you're not at the spending level of the 100th-ranked company, Subauru of America, a modest $108 million plus, you have a right to hold your head up.

- *Most companies ad budgets are far more modest.* The point is, *companies must acknowledge the limitations of their budgets.* Most $70-$100 million ad agencies would be pleased to compete for an account with a $20 million ad budget. It's when the $500,000 account wants $20 million level service that the wheel falls off. Everything's relative. All clients are entitled to good service. However, if your budget is $2 million, do not focus your search on agencies whose typical client budget is five times your budget and expect to be pleased with the results.

- *If your company has a regional management system and regional advertising, you may want an agency with offices corresponding to your locations.* But if all of your advertising is directed or coordinated by a single person or committee at one location, your agency should be working with that individual. The number of agency branch office locations is then irrelevant.

- *How many clients should an agency have?* As many as they can handle effectively. This question comes up because all clients want to feel they are important to their agencies—actually, that they are perhaps the agency's *most* important client. That's how it should be. Ask who and how many persons will be assigned to your account team and ask, too, what other accounts they are responsible for. Make your own determination as to your comfort level with the individuals and their workload. Obviously, some people have the capacity to handle more than others, but an account team that is spread thin and trying to do too much will have a negative impact on all clients involved, and if a member of the team leaves or is unavailable it could be a multiple disaster.

This is a point that comes up often in reviewing various aspects of the agency/client relationship: most everybody seems to believe that their business is different. Usually, this is not the case.

People are unique, but a creative director or copywriter is likely to employ the same process when working for a machine tool account as for a pharmaceutical company or a financial service client. A good biographer researches, organizes and outlines material before writing, whether the subject of the biography is a pilot, a statesman or a tap dancer. Similarly, ad agency professionals meet, review their research, strategize and plan a campaign based on data. Yes, the industries are different and the trade media different, but the process is usually the same. To the agency professional, this process is akin to doing homework and getting up to speed on the assignment.

It is widely accepted that a hospital would want to narrow its search for an ad agency to those agencies that had hospital advertising experience. This approach certainly is safe and serves to narrow the field, but it eliminates from consideration agencies that may have a lot to give in the way of creativity and service. A hospital is a service enterprise. An agency with experience in other service industries may well rise to the challenge and deliver a fresh perspective otherwise not offered.

Don't automatically rule out agencies because they aren't already working for your competitors or in your industry. With few exceptions, good agency people will learn what they need to know quickly and well if they really want your business.

Directories and Contacts

Now that you have a "profile" of the kind of agency you would like to hire—creative, research-oriented, local with a good media department—and a profile of your own account, where do you begin to look?

The first and best place to consult is the *Standard Directory of Advertising Agencies*, commonly called "The Agency Red Book." It is published by National Register Publishing Company (the address of which can be found in the *Sources and Resources* section of this book). "The Agency Red Book" is published three times each year and contains listings of some 5,000 advertising agencies— names, addresses, key personnel, areas of specialization, size, breakdown of billings and the roster of each agency's current clients. The listings are cross-referenced alphabetically, geographically and by billing classifications. Branch offices are listed if they exist. A sample page is reproduced here.[*] "The Agency Red Book" truly offers a wealth of comparison information.

Another source of agency information is your own staff. It is likely that among your advertising or marketing staff are people who have worked elsewhere at some time. What did they think of their former employer's advertising? Who did it? Who else's advertising do they

---

[*] By a curious coincidence, this page of "The Agency Redbook" shows the agency with which the author of this work is associated.

Exhibit 2–1: Sample Page from "The Agency Red Book"

WATTENMAKER ADVERTISING INC.—*Continued*

National Agency Associations: ABC—BPA

James Wattenmaker .... Pres.
Lois Adams .... Production Mgr.
Monica Wesolowski .... Media Dir.

Brookside Brand Div., Better Meat Products Co.,
 Cleveland, OH
Connors Bros., Inc., Westwood, MA
Gorton Corp., Gloucester, MA
Kohrman, Jackson & Krantz, Cleveland, OH
North Atlantic Seafood Assn., Cleveland, OH
St. Charles Group, Ft. Myers, FL
Telxon Corp., Akron, OH

001153-000

**WATTS & PAQUET COMMUNICATIONS
INC.**
**342 Commercial Ave., Palisades Park, NJ
07650**
Tel.: 201-585-5300

Employees: 15   Year Founded: 1985

Approx. Annual Billing: $5,000,000

Breakdown of Gross Billings by Media:
Newsp. $275,000; Mags. $4,160,000; Radio &
TV $125,000; Misc. $440,000

C.D. (Skip) Watts .... Pres.
James M. Paquet, Jr. .... Exec. V.P. & Creative
                                                            Dir.
Robert Lettiere .... Media Dir.
Acct. Execs.: C.D. Watts, J. Paquet, Charon
Maceri

Advanced Graphic Systems Non-Impact
 Printers
Allied Bendix Aerospace/Bendix Flight System
 Div. Aircraft Avionics, Flight & Engine Instru-
 ments, Color Displays, Flight Controls, Film &
 Digital Map Systems, Display Processors
Bobst Inc. Die-Cutters & Creasers
Bobst Champlain, Inc. Printing Presses
Bobst Registron. Tension & Register Controls
 for Printing Presses
Clark Aiken Matik. Unwind Stands, Rewinds &
 Sheeters
Gallus Inc. Printing Presses
Hishi Plastics U.S.A., Inc. Mfrs. of Heat Shrink-
 able Plastic Tubing
Integrated Converting Systems, Inc. Bus. Forms
 Printing Presses
Labelex Ltd. Label Expo '89; Tag, Tape & Label
 Trade Show
Leader Systems, Inc. Verification Systems; Bar
 Code
Liberty Machine Co., Inc., Paterson, NJ Coating
 & Laminating Machinery
Lipton, Thomas J., INc., Englewood Cliffs, NJ
 (Special Projects for Various Food Prods.)
Martin, S. A., Lyon, France. Corrugated
 Boxmaking Machy.
MetPath Health Services Inc., Fair Lawn, NJ
 Comprehensive Health Services to Physicians,
 Hospitals, Nursing Homes, HMO's, etc.
MetPath, Inc. Clinical Reference Lab.
Peters, W.H.K., Maschinenfabrik. Corrugators &
 Corrugating Equip.
Proofing Technologies Inc. Off-Press, Ink-On-
 Paper color Press Proofs
Ruesch, Ferd., AG. Printing Presses
Schuler Sales & Service Co. U.S. Distr. for
 Kolbus
Statewide Reports, Midland Park, NJ Financial
 Services
Thatcher Plastic Packaging. Plastic Packaging

•
003305-000

WEBB & ASSOCIATES, INC.
**3732 Mt. Diable Blvd., Ste. 360, Lafayette,
CA 94549**
Tel.: 415-283-1733
Telefax: 415-283-6293

Employees: 13   Year Founded: 1964

Approx. Annual Billing: $2,000,000

Breakdown of Gross Billings by Media:
Newsp. $900,000; Farm Publs. $55,000; Mags.
$125,000; Pub. Rels. $5,000; DM $5,000;
Outdoor $125,000; Radio $65,000;
Production $175,000; Fees $100,000;
Collateral $425,000; Misc. $20,000

John M. Webb .... Pres.
Thomas Bigford .... Exec. V.P.
J.M. Webb, III .... Sec. & Treas.
Nancy Savier .... Sr. Art. Dir.
Dianne Ehlers .... Pub. Rel. Dir.
Mary Bruzza .... Media Dir.
Sarah Jacobson .... Production Dir.

Acct. Execs.: John M. Webb, Sue Braaten-
Pardini, John M. Webb III

Citation Homes. Residential Construction
Diablo Pacific. Residential Construction
Fairhill Foods. Food Processing, Packaging
Grosvenor Properties. Residential/Comml.
 Construction
Kaiser Aerotech & Electronics
Loomis. Armored Car Services
Magnuson Corporation. Food Pckg. Equip.
Smith Companies, The. Residential Construc-
 tion
Store-It-Stores. Retail Cabinet Stores
Trilex. Residential Construction
W. S. I., Inc. Residential Construction

003307-000

WEBER COHN & RILEY, INC.
444 N. Michigan Ave., Chicago, IL 60611
Tel.: 312-527-4260
Telefax: 312-527-4273

Employees: 36   Year Founded: 1960

Approx. Annual Billing: $17,000,000

Breakdown of Gross Billings by Media:
Newsp. $2,300,000; Bus. Publs. $250,000;
Mags. $1,900,000; POP $50,000; Pub. Rels.
$2,000,000; DM $300,000; Outdoor $400,000;
Transit $250,000; Sls. Promo. $200,000; TV
$4,000,000; Radio $500,000; Yellow Pages
$50,000; Production $2,000,000; Fees
$2,000,000; Collateral $500,000; Cable TV
$150,000; Misc. $150,000

Ronald I. Cohn .... Chm.
James V. Riley .... Pres.
Joseph Marconi .... Exec. V.P.
Marc Michaelson .... V.P., Pub. Rels. Dir.
Ginny LaVone .... V.P.
Joan Scholl .... Media Dir.

Creative Dirs.: Chuck Welch, James Coudal

ĀAA Chicago Motor Club, Des Plaines, IL

ĀAA Travel Agency Illinois-Indiana
Brown's Chicken, Lombard, IL
Centel Cable Television, Des Plaines, IL
Chicago Cable Marketing Council, Chicago, IL
Chicago White Sox, Chicago, IL
GreatAmerican Federal Savings, Oak Park, IL
Group W Cable of Chicago, Chicago, IL
Heitman Financial, Chicago, IL
Intermedia Partners, San Francisco, CA
Mayfair Regent Hotel, Chicago, IL
Metrovision, Palos Hills, IL
Motel 6, Santa Barbara, CA
Northwestern Medical Faculty Foundation, Chi-
 cago, IL
Shifflet, D.K. & Associates, McLean, VA
Touche Ross, Chicago, IL
Travel Center Tours, Chicago, IL
United Audio Centers, Northbrook, IL
United Development, Oak Brook, IL
Van Kampen Merritt, Lisle, IL
Vein Clinics of America, Arlington Heights, IL
Washington National Insurance, Evanston, IL
York Furrier, Elmhurst, IL

•
003308-000
WEBER, GEIGER & KALAT, INC.
333 West First, Dayton, OH 45402
Tel.: 513-222-4683

                              Year Founded: 1947

H. A. Weber .... Pres.
Michael Woolley .... V.P. & Creative Dir.
Norman Vallone .... V.P. & Mktg. Dir.
John K. Webster .... V.P.
Charles Beers .... Art Dir.

Acct. Execs.: H. A. Weber, John K. Webster,
Norman Vallone, Charles Cooley

Apex. Div. Cooper Indus. Dayton, OH Fastening
 Tools, Universal Joints
Dupps Co., The. Germantown, OH Rendering
 Equip. for Meat & Poultry Processing
Electric Eel Manufacturing Co. Inc., Springfield,
 OH Sewer & Drain Cleaning Equip.
FWS/Schaefer, Frank W., Inc., Dayton, Ohio.
 Aluminum Melting & Holding Furnaces
Fusite Div., Emerson Electric Co., Cincinnati,
 OH Hermetic Terminals & Glass-to-Metal
 Sealing
Grandcor Inc., Dayton, OH Medical Prods.
Grandview & Southview Hospitals, Dayton, OH
Ground Power Div., Hobart Brothers Co., Troy,
 OH Aircraft Ground Power Equip.
Jeffrey Div. Dresser Industries, Woodruff, SC
 Processing Equip. for Mining, Chemical,
 Forest Prods. & Solid Waste
Joyce/Dayton Corp., Dayton, OH Railroad &
 Industrial Jacks and Automotive Lifts
McCauley Accessory Div., Cessna Aircraft Co.,
 Vandalia, OH Aircraft Propellers, Governors,
 Synchrophasers, De-Icing Systems
Perfecto Industries, Inc., Piqua, OH Coil
 Handling & Press Feeding Equip. for
 Metalworking Indus.
Roots Div., Dresser Industries, Connersville, IN
 Rotary Blower, Centrifugal Compressors
Sheffield Measurement Div., Warner & Swasey
 Co., Dayton, OH Dimensional Measurement
 Prods.
Wolf Machine Co., Cincinnati, OH Fabric Cutting
 Tools

003310-000

**WEBER & SORENSEN,
REKLAMEBUREAU A/S**
Frederiksgade 25, 8000 Aarhus, Denmark
Tel.: (06) 12 70 77

Employees: 26   Year Founded: 1879

National Agency Associations: EAAA

Approx. Annual Billing: $4,217,000

Breakdown of Gross Billings by Media:
Newsp. $1,603,000; Bus. Pubs. $257,000;
Mags. $460,000; Production $1,868,000;
Other $29,000

Flemming Emmering .... Fin.

Acct. Suprvs.: Jorgen Normark, Mariann Dalby
Buhl

010732-000

WEBSTER, HARRIS & SMITH, INC.
(See Dan Smith & Associates, Inc.)

•
003312-000

WEED ADVERTISING
1755 Park St., Naperville, IL 60563
Tel.: 708-717-0220

Employees: 20   Year Founded: 1979

Approx. Annual Billing: $6,000,000

Robert E. Weed .... Pres.
Elaine L. Weed .... Exec. V.P., Creative Dir.
Robert W. Mills .... Sr. V.P.
Paul Greenfield .... V.P.
Mary L. Mills .... Media Dir.
Grady Boles .... Acct. Supvr.

(Continued—next page)

697

• Updating information has been received directly from agency like? A major national advertiser or a local bank, department store, auto dealer, hotel or restaurant? Why do they like that advertising? Who does it?

The most-read trade publications, *Advertising Age* and *Adweek*, are both published weekly and are widely available. Each issue devotes considerable space to how various agencies are responding to developments in their own clients' industries, as well as presenting interviews or profiles of ad people at work.

One very direct line is your local newspaper. Most big city newspapers have a marketing column or a general interest column in their business sections. The person who writes that column has a very good fix on what agencies are active in what type of industries or service business, technical or retail or business-to-business accounts. Call the columnists and ask for a few names of possible contenders for your business.

Newspapers, television stations, radio stations and outdoor advertising companies each deal with dozens of agencies. A commercial, ad or a billboard that really triggers a strong impression is a good starting point. Call the particular media and ask which agency created the ad. You can also check National Register's *Directory of Advertisers* for all pertinent information on who handles the company's advertising. A professional agency will not only discuss the possibilities with a client but will suggest other agencies a client might want to meet with if the chemistry doesn't seem right. (Yes, even ad agencies turn down business.)

The trade publication *Adweek* accepts notices from advertisers conducting agency reviews, as do most newspaper marketing or business columnists. The downside of letting media people know of your search early on is that any number of agencies wishing to be considered will begin knocking at your door and lobbying for your attention. Good business judgement requires that you not rule out a "dark horse" who comes calling, but better business judgement requires that you not spend your every waking moment fending off advances from those with whom you do not wish to pursue a relationship. As is the case in other industries, ad agencies too will press for unwanted attention. This is another reason to name a coordinator or chairperson of your search committee, to receive and respond to agency inquiries.

This is also a time to consider a consultant. Many people in many businesses dismiss the consultant as "the guy who's out of work but owns a briefcase." Check the qualifications of a consultant as you would an accountant or lawyer. Acting as your agent, listening to your priorities and profiling your ideal agency's characteristics, a consultant can free an advertiser to continue doing business as usual during the early stages of the search. With a consultant developing a long list of possible contenders and handling the first round of communications, acting as a "screening agent," the client can remain both unencumbered and anonymous.

Lists

Whether acting independently or with a consultant, the next step is to fine-tune the long list. Some clients believe the first list should include virtually everyone who has either expressed an interest or looked like a possibility based on samples of their work viewed in the media, referrals and recommendations, solicitation letters received over time, recommendations from in-laws or directory listings. This approach, referred to as a "cattle call," wastes time, is impractical to pursue effectively and reflects poorly on the level of professionalism of the client.

A long list should never be longer than twelve agencies. More than that becomes unwieldy; they begin to blend together, like a stack of resumes after you've received the first dozen.

There are two exceptions to this recommendation: First, if none (or few) of the twelve makes a truly strong impression during the first pass, go on to include more—another five or six, perhaps. Second, be open to the dark horse. If an agency not on your list displays truly impressive or creative ways to get your attention, they have earned your consideration.

Solicitation Letter: Questionnaires

The next step is a qualifying letter and questionnaire. This, sent to the twelve or so names on your long list, is the agency's first chance to impress you. The impact of the first impression is neutralized: all agencies are now on a level playing field, the biggest and smallest. The presentation of their credentials on paper offers a wonderful opportunity for agencies to really impress prospective clients with examples of professionalism, competence and creative flair.

Unfortunately, most agencies at this stage play it safe by providing simple, succinct responses to your questions, again, much in the manner of a resume. The responses will all look pretty much alike. To what degree a client chooses to solicit pure data or examples of creativity is the client's own choice. Some respondents jump the gun and provide more than the client requests as a way of showing both style and an eagerness to win the business (imagine a beauty pageant entrant winking and blowing kisses at a judge). You must decide how you feel about this: to be hungry and eager to please is good; to be patronizing and unctuous is not.

Be specific in what you ask of agencies at this point. Because someone rushes ahead and shows speculative creative ideas before you've requested no more than qualifying data, don't give them the edge (or your business) over those who've responded with only what was requested.

Your letter (or that of your consultant) should be brief and should both offer and request specific information within a specific time. Here is an example of a letter, simple and direct:

*   *   *   *   *

Mr. Joseph Marconi
Executive Vice President
Weber Cohn & Riley
444 North Michigan Avenue
Chicago, IL 60640

Dear Mr. Marconi:

Our organization is now in the process of soliciting background information from agencies that could be candidates for our advertising
account. We are a midwest-based national account in the financial
services industry. Our annual advertising budget is approximately
$3.5 million.

If you are interested in being considered for our account, please
send your response to the attached questions to me by March 18.

Our Advertising Committee will review all responses received by that
date and invite a small number of agencies to present their capabilities in person. All agencies responding will be notified whether or not
we wish to see an in-person presentation. Our intention is to have
our new agency in place within sixty days.

If you have any questions, please feel free to call me at (312)527-
4260.

Sincerely,

A Prospective Client

*   *   *   *   *

Attached the to the letter should be the qualifying questionnaire. Here are three different examples for your consideration:

*   *   *   *   *

Example #1: *Agency Qualifying Questionnaire*

1. Who are you?
2. In 250 words or less, tell us why you think we should select you as our advertising agency.
3. If you care to, include a sample of your work.

Example #2: *Preliminary Questionnaire*

1. Agency name, address, city, state, zip, and telephone area code and number.
2. Name of parent organization or other owner/or headquarters city if outside of this area.
3. Name and title of principal new business contact person here.
4. Number of full-time employees here.
5. Estimated billing last year in this office.
6. Billing range: smallest client—largest client here.
7. Minimum billings or compensation guarantees required of new clients first year?
8. Areas of specialization or special expertise (product or service categories? retail? business-to-business? health care? direct response? other?)
9. Current active clients by company, brand and product.
10. The single most important advantage your agency has to offer a new company or new venture.
11. Additional information you feel would contribute to a prospective client's assessment of your capabilities.

Example #3: *Agency Questionnaire*

1. What have been the agency's local office annual billings for the last five years? (If not local, use head office billings.)

2. If the agency has other U.S. offices, what were the company's total annual billings in 19—?

3. What percentage of agency billings' growth is from new business, and what percentage is from existing business?

4. What is the range of ad budgets handled? Report mean and median budget level as well.

5. How many personnel (non-clerical) does the agency employ?

6. What has been the agency's turnover rate among account service personnel over the past five years?

7. What is the agency's current list of clients?

8. What is the agency's list of clients won or lost in the past year?

9. What has been the agency's growth rate over the last five years in number of clients? Similarly, how many have been lost in the last five years?

10. What services are available from the agency? Which are performed in-house, and which are subcontracted?

11. What experience does the agency have with clients in our industry?

12. How much of the agency's experience is with retail markets as compared to business-to-business markets?

13. Briefly describe the agency's most recent retail and business-to-business campaigns.

14. What were the agency's three most effective campaigns, and why were they considered most effective?

15. What methods of compensation are utilized (retainer verses hourly billing verses commission)?

16. Who are the individuals who would be assigned to our account, and what are their backgrounds?

*   *   *   *   *

In his book *Choosing an Advertising Agency*, William M. Weilbacher recommends getting the basic information and then getting into such areas as cost accounting, financial history, personnel development, and philosophy, among other things.

Why?

A comedian once said, "Comedy is funny but discussions about what is funny are not funny." An ad agency's people and skills are vastly more important than its accounting system or its philosophy, in terms of what they can do for you. Be suspicious of those who take themselves too seriously.

In the first example questionnaire, you ask (perhaps challenge) the agency to separate itself from a crowded field by demonstrating what one assumes to be an ad agency's singular or unique strength: being creative. You also afford yourself an opportunity to judge overall communication skill in the manner the presentation takes. Is it concise, informative, imaginative and a good business presentation separate and apart from its creative qualities? The good agencies, before responding to this type of request, will be forced to do some homework (or research) to try to determine where you are or have been, separately and relative to your competitors, before presenting themselves to you. Professionals who want your business have to strike a balance: be unique—even on the edge—and yet be close enough to your level of acceptability to not be summarily eliminated from consideration because they don't understand enough about how you think or work. If they make your list of finalists, they will then have to deal with the question of whether or not to present "spec" creative work. At this point you are looking simply for some "spark" that might indicate the presence of the qualities on your list. While your best business judgement says to be objective, do not be afraid of an emotional response. Sometimes the highest compliment you might pay an agency is that they seem like nice people to work with. You could pick someone for far worse reasons than that.

In example two, the questions are direct, simple and should provide you with a good picture to evaluate against the profile you have created. Again, be alert to the form the agency uses in responding. Look at the presentation of *their* cover letter. Do they send their response in a pocket folder? With a bound cover? What subtleties do they use relative to other respondents to make themselves seem unique?

Example three is a type used often—*too* often. It requests, through sixteen questions (some multi-part), not only more information than you need to make an intelligent decision, but information that is of dubious value. For instance, question number eight asks for the list of clients won or lost in the past year, but it doesn't reference "won" out of any number of presentations. One might get a very different opinion of an agency that won three accounts out of three or four presentations than of a shop that picked up six new accounts out of twenty-three presentations. Further, does one really determine the choice of an advertising agency by asking for a "report (of) mean and median budgets" of clients served? This example is an actual one sent out to request not simply a response but a "term paper." Obviously, it was prepared by someone far more concerned with the accumulation of statistical data than with the wise choice of a creative group of "nice people" with whom to work. Example three solicits a high-volume response but does not leave much room for a look at the personality of the agency.

Now that the letters have been sent and you are awaiting the return of your completed questionnaire, note the form of the response. Some agencies will reply on the very last day. Their theory is that, like the last name on the ballot, positioning has value. The last one in the door before it closes will be the one remembered best. Others will see that the response is hand-delivered, brought by messenger or by an overnight express service—typically a vehicle for special attention. While the timing and delivery of the response are less important than the quality or content, they do provide another indication of how much an agency wants your business as well as how they operate.

Quickly respond to those who don't make the cut. A phone call is a nice courtesy. A mailgram or messengered communication is a gesture of good grace. At least, a letter should be sent at the earliest possible time to those who have been eliminated from consideration.

Next comes the process of evaluating the responses to the questionnaires. One normally professes to be the heart and soul of fairness during this process, but, in all honesty, it isn't the case. Some agencies' names won't hit you right—not enough vowels, for instance. Others will conjure up recollections of urban fables (things you can't confirm or don't really remember the details of, but seem to remember hearing someone say that they heard from someone else), such as a particular agency having a very high turnover rate or *is* prolonging the payment of its bills.

Acknowledge that and get on with the process. Focus on those things that are truly important in getting good, effective advertising and a solid working relationship. Of course it is only good business to know who you are dealing with. The company you choose will be your *agent*, representing your company or firm, advancing your image.

Keep the emphasis where it belongs. Again, referring to William Weilbacher's criteria for evaluation, he raises some twenty points against which an agency might be evaluated. These include such items as whether or not the agency's management is "young and vigorous or seasoned and sedentary" and the financial history of the agency with a look at its profitability. With all respect to Mr. Weilbacher, who cares? Apart from raising the question "Are these guys about to go out of business?" their margin of profit should be of small concern to the client. Ditto their age: "young and vigorous" are no more automatically in tandem than are "seasoned and sedentary." Neither vigor nor laziness is the exclusive quality of any age group. Some advertising professionals are going strong past sixty, while others are burned-out by thirty.

Further, as long as the client receives bills on time, understands the charges and agrees the amounts are both fair and within budget, discussions of cost accounting systems draws attention from the real point of the relationship, which should be, as Chiat/Day/Mojo founder Jay Chiat likes to say, "to make good advertising." The agency's margin of profit, while it most certainly should be paramount to agency principals, shouldn't be a factor in the client's decision.

As the advertiser reads over the questionnaires, the real issues are:

1   Am I impressed with the way in which this agency has responded to the questionnaire in terms of timeliness and manner of presentation?

2   Am I impressed with the content of the response in terms of the tone, organization, quality and any examples of work submitted?

3   Did they give me what I asked for?

4   Does the tone of their communication suggest an emphasis on working for *my* best interests or showing me *theirs*?

5   How much do I feel they know about my business?

6   How much does it appear they have done any special "homework" on my account before responding?

7   Do I feel I get a sense of the "personality" of the agency more than what I learned from their listing in the directories?

8   Has anyone from the agency called with any questions or even an acknowledgement of the invitation to present?

9   Do I feel at this point that I would like to meet these people?

If none of your twelve (or so) respondents score highly against these points, there are two alternative courses to follow. One is to go back to the directories and other sources and solicit more agencies. The other choice is simply to contact the agencies on your original list to acknowledge that you don't feel you have enough of a sense of who they are and to request that they submit some (additional) samples of their work. Any agency worth its salt will use such a contact as an opportunity to sell their qualifications, *hard*. If they don't, you don't want them and it's on to the next name on the list.

In all likelihood, however, you will receive responses that impress you. Good advertising agencies are good because they know how to promote their clients' products and services. They should also possess the skills to promote themselves . . . and they do.

Pre-Presentation

You should be able to narrow your list of finalists for your account to four or five agencies. They should be notified by phone and a meeting scheduled for presentation. Be suspicious of an agency that does not take advantage of an offered *pre*-presentation meeting.

Two to three weeks is adequate time for an agency to prepare for a presentation, assuming you are not asking them to present "spec" creative work. The format or ground rules for the presentation meeting should be set down in writing to let each agency know what is expected of them.

It is hard to imagine that an agency being asked to pitch for new business wouldn't want to scout the prospective client in advance in a get-acquainted meeting. With all members of your search committee present, hold the meeting in your own offices and allow each agency sufficient time (an hour or so) to present its credentials.

This amounts to a virtual bringing-to-life of the listing directory and questionnaire response. At this meeting you should present your memo to the agency, stating those things they need to know to make an intelligent presentation to you:

1 Note the problems, questions or concerns you wish the agency to address in its presentation.

2 Identify who will represent the client and request the names and functions of those who will be present for the agency. Specifically ask that the persons who will be working day-to-day on the account be present.

3 Describe any constraints the agency must work under, such as corporate (or parent company) identity standards, governmental oversight or review and so on.

4 Offer specific information regarding budget limits, prior commitments of any portion of the budget, any other relationships (public relations agency, media buying service, consultants, research firm) and any research that either might be made available or considered in the presentation.

5 Be specific about deadlines for both agency selection and the introduction of new work.

At the pre-presentation meeting the client and prospective agency have an opportunity to size-up one another. Whether or not you believe in the value of first impressions or "gut feelings," don't underestimate the value of the unsaid word or the "vibrations."

Ron Cohn, Chairman of Weber Cohn & Riley, says that when sending out a packet of material to a new business prospect or meeting formally for the first time, his aim is to present not only a picture of professional competence, but to convey a sense that "these are nice people I'd like to meet and talk with over a cup of coffee."

Alan Goodman and Fred Seibert are partners in the highly successful New York advertising agency Fred/

Alan, Inc. They made their mark in advertising history as preeminent experts in knowing how to reach the highly prized "baby boomers." Comfortably excelling in their niche, Seibert offered his secret of success in a 1990 interview with *Manhattan inc.* magazine: "Have fun. Make money. Stand the people you work with." This last, a reference to clients.

Stand the people you work with. A bit glib, perhaps, but really profound in that in an advertising relationship, achieving success involves more than mutual admiration or respect; qualities that are hard to define on the checklist—just feeling comfortable working together.

An observation on first meetings. You go to a doctor; you know he's a doctor and he knows that you know; so he asks directly, "how can I help you?" A lawyer walks into the room and you and he know he's a lawyer, so he asks "What can I do for you?" Typically, the advertising man enters and you both know what he does, but instead of asking what he can do for you, he begins telling you how creative, brilliant, and successful he is with awards and offices on all the major planets . . . and, by the way here's what we think you should be doing to make your company more successful."

It's not entirely his fault. Many clients classify their agencies as "vendors" rather than professional resources. Furthermore, a client might think of itself as "hiring an ad agency" in the same way an employer hires an employee. The usual ritual has an employer saying, "Tell me something about yourself." The candidate then tries to shine and brag (without seeming to do so—except in the late 1980's, when arrogance was called "attitude" and for awhile was actually rather fashionable). That sort of pseudo-formal, patronizing approach has never encouraged either side to show the kinds of qualities that ultimately make for a successful match.

The best ad agencies (and, for that matter, the best prospective employees) begin a meeting by asking what you are looking for, then offer responses and ideas in terms of how they can provide what you need. Just as the best advertising will emphasize the benefits of the product to consumers, the best agency will emphasize the benefits of using that agency to a client.

When you engage the services of a lawyer, doctor, accountant—even a fitness coach—you do so because you have determined they possess a skill or expertise. *You* determine they're good on the basis of their recommendations, references and examples of their performance, not because they *told* you they were good.

In your first meeting, begin by telling the agency what you want to do and how much you have allocated to do it. Ask the agency to offer an example or two (case histories) of how they approached problems of this type with other clients and to summarize the results. The responses should offer you a great opportunity to judge both how the agency works and how it *thinks*—strategizes.

If the agency can offer clear, successful, and appropriate examples, you may be on to something. If they liken your situation to another that is a bit off the mark but offers an illustration of their talents, give them points for skill and creativity. If, however, you sense they've just come to do their stock dog-and-pony show without addressing your needs, you've gained valuable insight on the kind of agency you *don't* want: the kind that develops a generic creative campaign and then goes out looking for a client who might buy it.

Some might say that such exchanges of ideas don't belong in a first meeting—that they're reserved for presentations.

Nonsense.

Remember that the purpose of the pre-presentation meeting is to get acquainted and size-up one another. Upon hearing your objectives and budget, the agency people should ask if you've conducted any research or testing—any focus groups, internal organization surveys or competitive analysis. The client should attempt to determine how comfortable and confident they'll be with the agency people. Do they ask intelligent questions? Do they listen or just wait to talk? Simply, how's the *chemistry*?

The presentation meeting will be focused more formally on what the agency has to offer and will either build upon (reinforce) the rapport of the first meeting . . . or not.

The first meeting "leave behind" is a significant prop. Very surprisingly, many agencies, large and small, either don't have or don't use this device. The reason this is surprising is that the business of the agency is to promote and help sell its clients' product, yet it hasn't clearly packaged its *own* product for presentation. The competent agency professional should be able to offer you a five-minute (or less) verbal sketch of the agency. ("We're a twenty-eight-year old, medium size agency with full-service capabilities in-house. This packet includes our client list and some examples of our work. It should pretty much speak for itself in terms of creative execution and effectiveness.") When you have to explain why your work is good, it probably isn't. Good ads don't require explanation. In presenting a case history, it's appropriate to state the problem and show the advertising and media plan developed to meet it. But a good ad is a good ad, and an agency that's proud of its work and the results it achieved will make certain that work finds its way to you. The packet should also contain short biographic sketches or profiles of the agency's key personnel in all areas—management, creative, account service, media, research, sales promotion and public relations. The "leave-behind" is as simple or elaborate as the agency cares to make it, but always answers the questions, "Who are these people? Who are their clients? What kind of work do they do?" An expensively produced, glitzy piece might suggest the agency is big and successful, but may also indicate that they take themselves too seriously. The ad agency exists to package products, services and businesses to make them look their best, always themselves staying in the background. Flashy agencies with glitzy brochures don't lend themselves well to staying in the background.

Now . . . it's showtime! The agency review is the opening night on Broadway/all-or-nothing shot at winning the prospective client's heart—and account!

Usually, the bigger the agency, the bigger the presentation. Many agencies have not only business development personnel but full-time presentation teams, typically consisting of vice presidents whose duties are solely to handle presentations—superbly, with a grace and flair worthy of the theatre.

Sometimes it's all for nothing. All too often, the very exercise of the agency review is only that—an exercise—because the winner was selected before the first questionnaires were even mailed. Perhaps it was the agency that the client's new director of advertising worked with at his previous job. Perhaps it was someone he met at his club who has become an acquaintance, or someone with whom the client's top management sits on a local church or school board, or a relative. Whatever—for any or for no reason, the client knew which agency would get the business and maintained a charade in "the interests of fairness."

If you know who you want to hire from the outset, save a lot of people time and money (including yourself) and hire them. Very often companies that put up a front of not favoring friends or relatives or long-term relationships only end up working harder to conceal the favoritism, but it exists nonetheless. Favoritism doesn't necessarily mean the work won't be good or the fees not competitive. Sometimes, working with someone known and trusted for years, an agency will feel the pressure to do even better, just to dispel the cries of favoritism. The truest level of unfairness and unethical conduct is when a client allows an agency to commit its human and financial resources to enthusiastically compete for business that has already been promised elsewhere. The simple fact is that it happens all the time. Agencies will work nights and weekends, challenging their personnel to come up with the best and brightest ideas their capabilities will allow only to see the assignment go to a lesser light. To get the best from your agency, play fair right from the beginning.

In your get-acquainted meeting, you may approach the process from either of two directions: looking for ways in which the prospective agency looks singularly terrific or looking for negative elements that might help you eliminate candidates when other factors are equal.

We've used the word "chemistry." Before you view a presentation itself, do you think the agency people appear:

> too patronizing?
> too casual?
> arrogant?
> flashy?
> opinionated?
> insensitive?
> argumentative?
> pompous?
> too formal?
> bureaucratic?

*   *   *   *   *

One advertiser said an agency executive told him they had targeted his firm as a prospective client because they decided they wanted a client in that industry. To that individual the remark was arrogant, insensitive and pompous. It didn't put a value on the relationship or suggest a promise of great things ahead. Indeed *which* client in the industry seemed of small concern; it could just as well be another name in another industry on the agency's client list.

*   *   *   *   *

Give your business to someone who really wants it.

If that statement seems simpleminded, it's not. Some agencies will pursue accounts that may seem too small to bother with because they need the announcement that they'd won some new business just to counterbalance news of their recent lost accounts. Sometimes these accounts last only until bigger, better accounts come along. A national agency that normally wouldn't consider an account with annual media billings of less than $10 million courted and won a client with a $400,000 ad budget. The reason given was they had only one account in their Chicago office—the Chicago-based unit of an important national client. The agency didn't want to be labeled a "one-client shop" in town, so it approached the $400,000 client and said, despite the fact that they (the agency) were a large national operation worth a lot more than the client, they would accept the client's business.

Why didn't they go after a $10 million account as they theoretically should have?

We don't know.

We *do* know that the client was so flattered by the attention and the idea of being represented by a prestigious national agency that the smaller shops in town didn't have much of a chance.

How did it turn out?

Two years and several account people later, the company has changed marketing directors. Business is fair and the relationship continues because the agency wants more than one client and the client stills like the large agency's prestige. Despite the budget being about the same, a quick survey revealed no one could remember hearing or seeing one of the client's ads.

A frustrating truth of advertising is that sometimes a product or company is just so good, so hot or so much in demand it is hard to determine what impact, if any, its advertising is having.

William Weilbacher suggests some thirty reasons agencies don't make the cut, including:

- the agency is financially unstable
- the agency is not profitable
- the agency is top-heavy with salesmen
- the agency has no plan to perpetuate itself and its management skills

With all due respect, these are good things to look at when choosing a bank, but as the focus of an ad agency choice, they suggest someone doesn't have enough to do.

If an agency looks like it may be financially rocky, your hiring them just might correct that. Perhaps their financial troubles come from one or more clients who defaulted on payments or are habitually slow-paying accounts. Do you punish otherwise talented people for having clients who don't pay their bills? If business management isn't their strongest point, but they otherwise seem terrific, do you still want to eliminate them from consideration or do you want to try to work through this point?

Is the agency perhaps not profitable because of any particular reason? Do we care as long as we get good work and good service at competitive rates?

Regarding plans to perpetuate management skills, shouldn't we leave someone else's job to someone else and just worry about the quality of service we receive for our money?

What is it we are looking for?

Just as an adequate questionnaire could have consisted of three questions, separating a few from many candidates can be achieved on the basis of a few simple criteria:

1   Do they seem to know their business and produce good advertising?

2   Do they understand or appear capable of understanding *my* business?

3   Are they honest? (Checking with their clients or financial references can answer that easily).

4 Do I feel comfortable around them and do I have confidence in them?

If all of your candidates get a "yes" on all accounts, enjoy suffering this embarrassment of riches and await their more formalized presentations to help you make your choice.

Much of how successful these presentations are will be determined by your adherence to the prior suggestions of keeping the size of your committee small and the list of finalists short. Here's why:

- You want to see each of the agencies at their absolute best. That means you should view each of their presentations in *their* offices. You should see their offices anyway, as it will help you form (or confirm) your opinion of who they are and how they work. Too many people on your side makes travel, scheduling, viewing and deciding all tougher than it needs to be. That's a reason to keep your committee few in numbers.

- Having to visit many locations is tiring, time consuming, a real hassle and, after a point, places tend to run together (". . . was the agency with the fruit on the table the one with the orange conference room chairs?"). *Selecting the best agency is the job.* By cutting corners and not inconveniencing yourself, you won't be in any way better positioned to make that choice.

Some clients have said that it's easier for the client to stay in one place and make the agency come to them (after all, it's the agency who is on the receiving end of the budget). Besides, seeing all contenders presenting in the same conference room puts them all on an equal footing at the start. After that, it's up to them.

Wrong on both counts.

First, "what's easier for the client" is to do what ultimately helps the client make the best, most informed decision. That means giving your finalists every opportunity to be as relaxed as they can be (home court advantage) and have whatever resources they need available to them. Further, meetings of any type held in client offices are rarely free of interruptions, whether brief important phone calls or sudden meetings with someone who "just needs to see you for a minute." This is terribly unfair to the agency giving the presentation. It breaks the momentum and negates the very fairness you're attempting to assure.

Another reason why having everyone present in the same place doesn't assure objectivity or fairness is that differences exist from the moment the presenters arrive. One group may consist of two people using photos on easels; another may have four people with a video reel and slides; another might have several people, all men or all women or a team of men and women of varying ages doing a multi-media pitch (something for everybody). The people presenting will be different and the work they show will be different. And if you view two presentations in the morning and another one or two in the afternoon (perhaps after a heavy lunch) you are not going to be looking at them in any kind of objectivity just because of the room.

Sometimes, this issue arises: a very busy CEO wants to have the final say, and you can't ask him or her to run all over town visiting ad agencies.

Well, you needn't. If your CEO wants to have the last word, arrange a separate meeting with the agency in your offices to bless the union *after* you've made the selection. As all good books on the subject tell us, a first-class chief executive officer vests authority and confidence in the person who will be responsible for choosing and selecting a great team in this case, the ad or marketing VP or director. If that confidence isn't there, that person has more to worry about than choosing an ad agency.

If your candidates are nice people who really want your business, they're going to be at least a little nervous (certainly, at least eager to please). Don't compound the anxiety. Do all you can to see them at their best. It's to *your* benefit.

If possible, schedule each agency's presentation on a different but successive day. There's much superstition about going first or last being an advantage. The fact is that the *real* advantage is in being the only one presenting. It may seem harder on your team to spread things out, but it really is better for both sides for you to separate the sessions as a way of seeing each agency's "personality."

Schedule presentations in the morning. Allow each agency ninety minutes: sixty minutes for the presentation, thirty minutes for conversation and questions.

New business is the lifeblood of advertising agencies. This is a creative business that can never afford to stand still. Even working for the same clients and with high profitability, tastes change, markets expand and contract. Freshness is always the order of the day. New business presentations are synonymous with that freshness. A new name in the agency, a new challenge. It is stimulating, exciting, invigorating. All the juices are flowing and the managers know that the disappointment their team will feel if they don't land the account is a good thing. It means they've put a lot of themselves into preparing for this presentation and they are pumped up. That quality is an "edge." When it's missing the work shows it. The presentation team knows it and the result is the difference between okay and terrific.

The time and place are set and the stopwatch is running. The agency teams have taken deep breaths, cleared their throats and stepped forward into the spotlight.

We know about the *chemistry*—that *who* presents and *how* can be every bit as important as the substance of the presentation. Are you hearing from the agency founder? Its senior management? The "ace presenter" or the people you will be working with? They've got an hour. How much of the time do they spend talking about themselves and how much about what they propose to do for you?

How much time do they spend talking about their philosophy? How important is their philosophy to you? If it is an important consideration, is what you hear something you can relate to—does it have a *relevance* to your business?

How organized is this presentation? Does it appear that the agency has outlined its presentation and orchestrated its people and visuals to allocate adequate time for:

- introductory remarks—their history, structure, philosophy
- their situation analysis
- objectives of their proposal
- strategies for achieving objectives—research, media, other
- recommendations—including budgets and fees
- explanation of compensation arrangements
- conversation and questions?

Veteran advertising man Whit Hobbs writing in the trade magazine *Adweek* advocates each search committee member using a score sheet and rating the agency from one to ten on a series of important categories such as:

- the scope of the agency
- attitude
- creativity
- chemistry

Focus on such considerations as, "Do they *really* want our business?" "Are they our kind of people?" "Will we be able to work together?"

Some clients absolutely leave it to the agency to present cold. Tell us what we need to do. Tell us how much we need to spend. Tell us something we don't already know. *Impress* us.

It is then up to the agency, presumably having asked the right questions, listened and done their homework, to organize a buttoned-up hour from top to bottom: State a premise. Validate the premise. Identify the problem. Propose the solution. Some will choose to lecture, others to dazzle with props and showmanship.

Often clients will offer the premise themselves, providing the agency with a specific stated challenge and asking only for the response ("If you were our agency, how would you address . . . ?").

Your evaluation then should note the agency's degree of:

- organizational skill demonstrated
- research employed
- ego
- creativity
- fiscal responsibility (a high-brow term meaning, "Did they think this through seriously and can we afford their solution?")

Frequently, a client will say the presentation is not to include any speculative creative work. Creative solutions, suggestions and recommendations are expected, but an artistic execution of those ideas is expensive and time consuming. Not every candidate will win the account. It is, therefore, a gesture of courtesy and consideration that the client stipulates, "No speculative creative, please."

The agencies then, of course, go on to produce spec creative work anyway and risk the out-of-pocket costs on the chance that if they do *not* show spec work, but a competitor (or worse, *competitors*) do, they will be at a disadvantage and appear to not want the account as much as the other agencies do. So typically, even though the client may say not to do it, clients and agencies in most cases expect spec work to be shown.

It is the best way, ultimately, to choose an agency. The adage is that the creative work is what wins the account and the service is what keeps it (and we will repeat this a few times for emphasis). Of course an agency can (and normally does) show its best creative work for its other clients, explaining how it worked to address and solve that client's problems. But since the underlying question in a new business situation is what the agency will do for *you*, the other client's work, no matter how strong or how many awards it's won, won't be as important as the idea and strategy (with media plan) supported by spec creative work.

Some clients, recognizing this fact, graciously offer a token amount to each finalist to cover spec work. So whether or not you choose to state the premise or leave the whole show to the agency and whether or not you ask for or expect spec work, here are some things to look for in evaluating your prospective agency:

1 Were they confident and professional?

2 If you gave them specific guidelines, did they stay within them?

3 Did they utilize the information from the preliminary meeting?

4 Was the presentation "slick" or "canned" (like a presentation that might just as easily be—and likely is—given to any other prospective client)?

5 Did they stay focused on *your* company and problems or on *their* history and successes?

6 Did they offer research and/or media recommendations?

7 How did they handle the issue of budgets, compensation and fees?

8 Did you get to meet and question the people who would work with you or only the "new business" team of star presenters?

9   How did they handle questions?

10   How would you rate the agency and its people overall?

11   Did they leave behind a presentation book that summarized what you saw and anticipated your questions?

The Presentation Book

The presentation book is of unique importance. Sometimes it's a series of sheets in a pocket folder, sometimes a bound book. *Always* it is a way for you to judge the depth and thought—the *scope*, as Whit Hobbs called it—of an agency when the smiles, slides and theatrics of the presentation have faded from memory. A very good presenter can make a more modest idea come to life (just as a strong celebrity endorser/presenter might put some extra sizzle in an otherwise just "okay" TV, radio or print ad). Production techniques such as art, design, photography, lighting or sound effects may make a much more memorable presentation, but the leave-behind presentation *book* will tell you how the agency sells itself and its ideas when it can't be there in person—much like the way your advertising will have to create an impact on its target audience.

An agency's skill in production is of major importance. A very good idea or message poorly executed results in advertising that is anywhere from mediocre to bad. Viewing the presentation, the creative samples and the agency reel will show you examples of production skills and capabilities. The book demonstrates the business side of the agency, its packaging and organizing abilities. It may not include creative, but it definitely should include the recommendations, their justification and costs.

After you have heard from each of the finalists, thank them for their efforts and tell them when you expect to make your decision. Spare them the twenty-four-hour vigil at the telephone.

Schedule a search committee meeting at your office and, after every member of the committee has checked his or her score sheet, vote. This is the time for discussion—pros, cons—as this debate could mean not only the difference between choices A or B, but between a good working relationship or a poor one.

In case of a tie, invite a neutral party—someone from senior management—to break the tie by reviewing the presentation books and making a choice. As this person hasn't seen the presentation, and is judging without benefit of stage presence and props and slides, the raw essence of the presentation will have to carry its own tune.

With your selection made, it is a generous gesture to phone those not chosen and thank them again, before calling to congratulate your new agency on being selected.

An additional optional gesture is to send a plant or flower arrangement of congratulations to the winner with a note expressing appreciation for all that went into their presentation. It's a nice first step to getting the best and the most from your new ad agency relationship.

To review:

1   Keep your search committee small (including advertising director and/or a consultant).

2   Create a long list of a dozen or so agencies from directories, referrals and recommendations.

3   Prepare and mail a questionnaire to the "Lucky 12."

4   Evaluate responses and shorten your list to three to five finalists.

5   Have get-acquainted meetings at your offices with each of the finalists and tell them what your needs, objectives, budgets and limitations are.

6   Schedule presentation meetings *at the agencies*.

7   Review each presentation on a separate day if possible.

8   Evaluate each presentation on paper according to an agreed criteria.

9   Meet with your committee to compare written evaluations. Discuss strengths and weaknesses of the candidates.

10   Phone the agencies you did not select and thank them for their efforts, before calling your new agency with the good news.

11   (Optional) Send your agency a congratulatory flower arrangement.

The Letter of Agreement or Contract

Unlike other businesses where so much money is involved, in advertising, the rule regarding contracts is that there is no rule. Some clients want a detailed contract specifying who will be responsible for what, at what cost and at what terms. Other clients are satisfied with a handshake and a verbal agreement.

To quote the late Richard J. Daley, who was the political boss and mayor of Chicago for twenty years, "A verbal agreement isn't worth the paper it's written on."

Respect, understanding, professionalism, and integrity are essential ingredients in the agency/client relationship. Like a pre-marital agreement, a contract implies "You can count on me, but just in case . . ."

Surveys of ad agencies indicate that about half of them have formal contracts with their clients and about another quarter of them have some less formal-type of letter of agreement. The others have a handshake and a prayer that everyone remembers what was promised.

To get the relationship off on the best possible footing, both sides want only the most overt shows of good-

will, but a money-back guarantee is always in writing because the fixing of it to paper says, "Let there be no mis-
understanding about the degree of my commitment."

Many, if not most, relationships run into trouble because of misunderstandings; few because of actual fraud
or misrepresentation.

Lawyers tend to take all the fun and warmth out of
the proceedings. Fun and warmth are two of the things
ad agencies like to have in their client relationships. Lawyers also are the natural enemies of ad agencies. They insist on "protecting" advertisers by insisting that ads carry
obvious information that insults the audience's intelligence, such as "your mileage may vary," "void where
prohibited," and the ever-popular "call for and read the
prospectus carefully before you invest or send money."
(They feel this is necessary because people may send
money without knowing what they're buying.)

Contracts are neither funny nor fun to read; they
convey a heaviness of tone that can make even the most
easygoing people quite uncomfortable. If your company
is heavily invested in lawyers and saddled with a policy
that requires contracts for important service relationships,
this debate may be moot. If, on the other hand, your
company's policy is simply to establish trusting relationships, no matter how informal the arrangement, let's take
a moment to discuss why neither of these extreme positions is much better or worse than the other.

First, some type of an agreement needs to exist. Both
sides are in business; people come and go, and newcom-
ers are often unfamiliar with the understandings that
guided the relationship in the past. This is perhaps the
strongest reason to commit something to paper—to begin
clearly defining guidelines of who will be responsible for
what.

Lawyers will argue that a contract should exist to address such considerations as compensation, liability, conflicts, the term of the relationship and under what conditions the relationship might be terminated.

However, the good advertising agency normally provides its clients with far more than any contract requires. For example, while an agency purchasing media time and space for its client will make the buy and take its fee or commission, the *good* agency negotiates media buys that provide the client maximum savings while also negotiating for number of bonuses ranging from free ads to merchandising support. Rarely (if ever) are such arrangements mentioned in a contract because, typically, the agency receives no additional compensation for ads run at no charge or for merchandising deals, nor can they be guaranteed. As they result from negotiation, there is no way to anticipate the result—it's just what good agencies do as a part of the service arrangement that tries to get the most for their clients. Let a "memorandum of agreement" serve to satisfy the contractual concerns of your legal department while setting the guidelines for your working relationship.

The agency, upon being chosen, should prepare the memo for the client's review. It should be direct but friendly: "Thank you for your confidence. Just to be certain we begin on the right note, here is a summary of points on which we believe it is important we are in agreement . . ."

The agency then should list those issues to which it wants to make certain the client agrees. They should be numbered for ease of future reference, discussion or revision. The list might be something like this:

1   The agency will officially become your agency of record effective [date].

2   Either party may terminate this relationship upon written notice provided sixty days in advance of a termination date.

3   The agency will act as your media buyer, is authorized to pay for such media within the limits of the approved media plan ad budget and will invoice you accordingly, retaining the usual and customary media com-

mission (typically 15 percent, but subject to negotiation under other fee or compensation arrangements).

4 The agency will undertake research on your behalf, with written prior approval to form and costs.

5 You agree to reimburse the agency for expenses incurred on your behalf, provided those expenses were approved by you in advance. This typically includes such products or services as art, photography, design, typesetting film and related production expenses. An amount equal to the standard 15 percent commission will be added. Out-of-pocket expenses, such as air freight, messengers, travel and entertainment will be invoiced without service charge.

6 The agency agrees not to undertake advertising on behalf of anyone who might be considered your competitor.

7 The agency will provide copies of all outside suppliers invoices relating to your projects, if requested, as supporting attachments to our invoices.

8 The agency agrees to take responsibility for obtaining the necessary rights and releases for the use of art and talent.

9 You agree that information provided the agency by you for use in advertising is true and correct and you agree to hold the agency not responsible for the correctness of this information.

10 Assuming a standard commission arrangement, the agency agrees to provide account and creative services, art and production supervision, media planning/purchasing and consulting for a fee not to exceed the equivalent of 15 percent of the agreed budget for media.

11 Assuming a fee compensation arrangement, the agency will provide a range of account, creative and related services at an agreed upon fee.

There may be other points you will want to include such as assuring confidentiality in the use of proprietary information or specific reporting or supervising relationships.

Conclude the memo with words to this effect: If this correctly reflects your understanding of our working relationship, please sign a copy of this memo and return it to me, or call if any corrections are needed."

The idea is to maintain a comfortable, respectful, trusting relationship. The agency is being hired to create and manage a campaign that will help the company grow and prosper. The more rigidity in the relationship, the more tension, the more likely the quality of the resulting work will suffer.

Your "letter of agreement" should be just that— "agreement." When parties agree, so the story goes, everything works out fine.

Conflicts

From the moment the agency review begins, throughout the process and for the entire duration of the client/agency relationship, *conflicts* will be discussed.

There are some things about which some people make too much. Almost any time a client selects an ad agency, the subject of conflicts of interest is raised and normally ends up getting a paragraph or two in the letter of agreement. This is okay. It makes a point of stating the obvious: the client objects to its agency also representing the client's competitor, so the agency promises not to do so.

No sane agency chief would even fantasize about representing both Ford and Chevrolet. Burger King and Wendy's. *Time* and *Newsweek*. Clients wouldn't have it and it just wouldn't be considered, by anyone.

In the mid-1980's "merger mania" hit the ad industry. Omnicom was formed by three of the industry's largest agencies, while Saatchi & Saatchi seemed to by buying agencies as fast as they could find their phone numbers in the Agency Red Book. Others were just as busy. As agencies merged many accounts and their agencies parted company. The Saatchis saw some $500 million worth of business move because the newly combined shops had conflicts. But did they?

When the Chicago office of a national agency handles an account and the Los Angeles or Atlanta office of the same parent agency handles the business of a competitor, is that a problem for anyone as long as the two pledge not to share information? If different creative teams and different media planners and buyers work independently of one another, the net effect is the same as if the two clients used two separate agencies.

Naive? Not at all. Agencies frequently will assign two (or more) creative teams to develop campaigns for the same client. The teams work quite independent of each other, not trading ideas or research and, in effect, *competing* to produce the best work.

It is really not the agency, but the *people* working on the client's advertising who are the key element. Yes, agency media strength and research capabilities are valuable resources, but a team that doesn't have the right combination of talent, skill and personality (that *chemistry* again) will not be a strong team for the client, no matter what the size or reputation of the agency.

There are other instances where conflicts are overemphasized. For example, when an agency represents both a bank and a financial services firm. They are structured differently, but both offer investment products. One wants the customer's money in certificates of deposit, the other in mutual funds. Both are paying similar interest rates. Some agencies and clients would consider this a conflict. Others would not.

In several cities the same local agency will handle media buying for more than one Hollywood movie studio. Obviously these clients are competing for the same moviegoer's ticket price on Saturday night, yet the clients' position is "get our spots on TV and radio and our ads in the paper and you've done your job for us."

Carried to the absurd, all clients are conflicting: the real estate developer and the yacht manufacturer would not consider themselves competitors (nor would an agency that might have both as clients), yet both are asking the prospective customer to purchase a comparably priced investment/possession; the clothing store and the bicycle shop both want the customer in the same target group to make that $300 or $400 (or more) purchase. Are they competing? Hallmark cards fired its agency because the agency also handled a telephone company. Hallmark saw a conflict.

David Ogilvy advises "If I were you, I would think twice about firing my agency when it committed bigamy; another agency might not give you such good advertising."

Mr. Ogilvy's firm, Ogilvy and Mather, is owned by WPP Group. So is J. Walter Thompson. Technically, clients of the two agencies who were competitors would pose a conflict of interest. Over the years, these two giants have competed aggressively for the same account. If a prospective client no longer encouraged them to do so, it would be the client's loss.

Roderick White, in his book *Advertising—What It Is and How To Do It*, writes "The argument about conflicting accounts is an old one and 'conflict' is open to numerous interpretations. In general, in my experience, conflict lies chiefly in the eyes of the clients, but agencies are obsessed with it...what I can only describe as corporate possessiveness and hypersensitivity justifies the sort of policy that prevents an international agency which handles Gillette razor business in one country from handling Schick razor business in any other country."

When addressing the conflict problem Foote, Cone & Belding's former Chairman John O'Toole notes, "curiously enough, companies do not impose such rigorous loyalty tests on their law firms, banks or accounting companies—just their advertising agencies."

The true conflicts are obvious—the same people working for directly competing enterprises in the same market. But as in every other aspect of the relationship, the overriding consideration is trust. When the people who will be working together on both sides decide they *really* want to get together to develop and run good advertising that works, the trust and integrity that comes with the relationship makes whoever else they work for (or with) irrelevant. Conversely, if you don't trust your agency is committed to giving you their absolute best efforts, the list of reasons why becomes only a talking point in a relationship that probably shouldn't continue.

A Perfect Fit: Does the Size of Your Ad Agency Matter?

"Creative" is said to be, at various times, the only, the main, the pivotal or at least the decisive factor in the choice of an advertising agency. It's interesting then to see the lengths to which some agencies go to bring themselves to your attention in the most uncreative ways.

For instance, consider the matter of size in determining the agency you choose.

It shouldn't take a genius to conclude that if you are a large operation with specific needs in a number of cities, regions or countries, a one-person or small shop couldn't give you what you need. Similarly, of course, a smaller company can't afford to carry the costs associated with retaining a large, full-service agency. Just as in buying a suit that fits you properly, you start by looking at the size, your agency relationship too might begin with a size check. This also presents an opportunity to see up front how some agencies think.

One agency sent its prospective client fish.

On the first day a very large fish bowl was delivered to the client's office. It contained one small goldfish.

Day two, a much smaller bowl arrived by messenger. It contained one fish, which appeared to nearly fill the bowl.

If you couldn't guess by now, the third day brought a fish and bowl which looked just right for each other and a note summarizing the whole idea of the three days of deliveries was to show the analogy of how too big for one or too small for another wasn't right. Just right was right.

Little fish, big pond; big fish, little pond.

Reportedly the agency which spent its new business development budget at the local pet shop didn't get the account. It got the prospective client's interest . . . and ultimately its annoyance. Picture the office manager wondering what to do with three bowls of fish nobody asked for.

Also interesting are reports allegedly identifying the agency. Four mid-size agencies are credited with the stunt. Did they *all* do it at varying times? Was the credit for the idea mistakenly awarded? Is the whole thing folklore and just to prove a point?

Answers: it really happened. More than once. And *that's* a big part of the point. The agency people didn't determine how to approach the company in a way that told the company, "This would be a good match."

Perhaps a mention in a meeting or a memo, suggesting the agency had done its homework, simply saying "we're the right size for you," would have been enough. Perhaps a list of satisfied clients of roughly the same size as the prospective client would have made the point dramatically enough and conjured up images associating the agency with successful campaigns.

Then again, maybe some discussion of this point before any theatrics would have suggested both the client and agency were ready to take some chances. Frequently, larger agencies will take accounts it hopes to "grow" during long relationships. ("You're a half-million now, but in five years, you'll be a $4 million account and we have the time and staff to work with you.")

The other side of this is large companies giving smaller agencies a chance. The "hungry" young shop may offer both a creative edge and a willingness to provide excellent service that shouldn't be dismissed without consideration.

Remember above all your agency is not to be viewed as a corporation but as people, particularly the people who will work on your account.

Are they smart? Do they listen? Do they understand anything about your business, your objectives, your industry or your limitations? What do they know about your competition?

There are no guarantees that the larger agency, because it employs *more* people, will give you *brighter* people or more intelligence in the management of your account. The agency's size effects the depth of its resources and often (though not always) its media power, but not its talent. Without pushing the obvious too far, the simple fact is that talent and intelligence are not the exclusive commodities of the large, successful agencies or the small, hungry or fresh shops. As in your choice of a doctor, lawyer or accountant, talent is where you find it. Don't be blinded by the size of the billings, office space or the number of names on the door.

Is big better?

Obviously, some people think so.

Omnicom was formed out of the consolidation of three already large successful agencies—BBDO, Needham, Harper and Doyle, Dane, Bernbach. Their clients, which include major soft drink and automobile manufacturers, obviously told them this new, bigger entity was good for all of them. Or, at least, okay with them.

The Saatchi Brothers and WPP Group, both headquartered in London, obviously convinced their clients that big is better as they try to achieve "global power" in buying media.

There certainly is no debate that a huge client with global interests will likely require the time and resources a small shop couldn't provide.

Yet, it's fascinating to see how some agencies appeared to become "hot shops" virtually overnight because their creative strength found outlets with clients who broke from the traditional, predictable choices of established agencies and gave them an opportunity.

Both Nike and Apple Computer chose the little known Los Angeles agency Chiat/Day. Hugely successful campaigns put the agency in contention for Nissan Motor's $100-million account in 1988—which it won. Only a few years earlier, the auto giant would have asked "Chiat who?"

Fallon McElligot and Rice, a creatively oriented Minneapolis agency, also emerged as a "hot shop" of the 1980's, winning challenging, important national accounts such as Chicago financial giant Continental Bank and others over better-known, larger national agencies. The resulting work won numerous awards and much attention. And much more business.

Hal Riney & Partners was spun-off from the San Francisco offices of global agency Ogilvy & Mather and through such successes as the Bartles & James wine cooler campaign became instantly a national "hot agency" and a contender (and winner) in GM's Saturn review. A new car launch would be a major coup for any agency, but is particularly noteworthy when the agency is young and thought to not yet be a major contender.

One must assume the account was won on creative strength since the agency only a few months later ran ads in trade papers asking for creative proposals to utilize Saturn's $100 million media budget. Or it could have all just been part of a strategy.

So what does this tell us? Several things:

1   If Nissan could pick Chiat and General Motors could pick Riney, then one should no longer assume big ac-

counts need big agencies. Or at least we should reject the idea that a smaller shop can't put together a team capable of handling large accounts.

2   The important consideration is talent—not size or location—with companies that once would have headed straight for Madison Avenue now looking at Los Angeles, Minneapolis, San Francisco, Boston or Milwaukee.

3   While the giants such as BBDO, Ogilvy, Burnett, J. Walter Thompson and Foote Cone & Belding still produce some excellent work, they are no longer the exclusive, obvious choices for large account reviews.

4   With new generations of managers comes an end to the old rules. Just as Brooks Brothers once was the rule in board rooms where we now find Ralph Lauren or Georgio Armani, today's managers seek to establish new relationships without the narrow parameters of the past.

Tony Benjamin, executive vice president/creative director of the New York agency Friedman Benjamin Advertising, offers "Ten Reasons to Think Small" when selecting an agency:

1   You get better creative.

2   Small agencies are less expensive.

3   Substance over surface (meaning ideas are presented without excessive production treatment).

4   Clients are more important to small shops.

5   At small agencies, people aren't afraid to get their hands dirty (willing to handle such things as collateral and direct mail that large agencies usually don't want).

6   Small shops are "apolitical," with a staff too busy for corporate politics.

7   Small shops are faster.

8   Small shops are friendlier.

9   Small shops make a client's money go further.

10   Small agencies need every client.

Mr. Benjamin notes that it amazes him "when $1-5 million clients go to agencies that bill $500 million . . . the agency at first will promise you the world, but the reality is that big agencies can't afford little clients." If a client represents 1 percent of the agency's salary pool, what's the likelihood of their getting more than 1 percent of the agency's time or talent? The point is valid and certainly should be considered. How important can a $2 million account be to a $500 million agency? A lot less important than it would be to a $15-20 million agency. Yet such competition occurs often and it's usually the small agencies that lose out—after the client, that is.

Large agencies often will suffer a losing streak. A major account leaves. Maybe several accounts, large or small leave. The agency needs a morale boost. It needs to announce it's not slipping. It needs new business—*any* new business. So it goes after an account that it knows full well won't be around for the long haul, but may be a good "name" to announce it has picked up. The prospective client is flattered that such a large and prestigious ad agency would want to work for it. The small to mid-size agencies groan in despair knowing they'll not only be pitching against the larger agency's prestige, but against a new business machine that does nothing but present— very, very well—before (usually) turning the new account over to a group of fresh young recruits for servicing.

And, in all fairness, sometimes the recruits are very talented and everything works. Not often, but sometimes.

The simple fact is, the size mix should be right. The client should be important to the agency not just because that's the job, but because it represents a significant enough percentage of income to be worth the time and interest of the agency's creative and management professionals.

Only the right size agency can afford to really service a client correctly, building a solid relationship of senior management to senior management.

To rank agencies by size, that is by media billings, is somewhat arbitrary, but this is a reasonably acceptable break:

very small or specialty shop	under $12 million
small agencies	$12-80 million
medium size agencies	$80-300 million
large agencies	$300 million +

Typically, a good fit has your advertising budget at between 8 percent and 20 percent of the agency's billings, but that number is not chiseled in stone. Many successful relationships have existed beyond these parameters because size is only one factor to be considered in your agency relationship. Some other considerations are:

1 *Account conflicts.* This is important for the most obvious reasons. An agency shouldn't and can't represent two competing businesses nationally or in the same market. This is a clear point with regard to the obvious conflicts (such as between radio stations or food chains or retailers and their competitor's stores in the same town), but it is often more difficult to determine *indirect* conflicts. Is a bank a competitor of a mutual fund company? Is a health insurer a conflict with a life insurance company? A cable TV company with a publication whose parent company may own cable TV stations in other markets? These are all questions the agency must resolve with all parties before entering into potentially conflicting agreements.

2 *Locations.* Today's modern communication systems make it possible to work closely with a client even if that client is in another city. Phone, fax and Federal Express are all convenient, cost-effective and efficient business tools. Yet many companies prefer frequent face-to-face meetings, which can cut into a budget dramatically if the agency doesn't have an office nearby.

3   *Agency history and reputation.* Whether it is a newly incorporated venture or a shop several generations old, a client should be comfortable with an agency's reputation. Are awards important? If so, how do they measure up? How many awards? How recently won? Who was responsible? Is the principal of the agency a creative type or a manager? What's been the agency's record of growing and keeping both accounts and talent?

4   *Overall Capabilities.* How much is in-house and what's "farmed out?" Does the agency have on-staff art directors, copywriters, creative directors, media planners, keyliners, typesetters, a research team? While these are all important considerations, the extent of their importance to each individual client will be different. Going outside for research, audio-visual or print production can often mean great cost efficiencies. Depending on who they are, how many and what they do and how they are utilized determines the difference between agency "capabilities" and "overhead."

5   *Chemistry.* If agency and client personnel can't look each other in the eye, laugh together and just generally feel good about each other, it doesn't matter how many offices the agency has, where they are located, how many art directors they employ and all the rest—chemistry is essential.

6   *Creative.* This is listed last, but is normally the first thing a client looks at in selecting an agency. Few words are as overused as *creative*, but how an agency conceives and executes its ideas, the media it selects and its overall presentation of its work constitute the most important factors in distinguishing one agency from another. Research, account service and media planning and management are of critical importance. Yet it is the creative product that gets the attention, and rightly so.

Some agencies will say they are "creatively-driven," others stress the "integrated" approach, combining a number of communications disciplines. Any and all attempts by an agency to distinguish itself from its competition should be viewed as a plus for a client. That agency would seek the same kind of strategic and philosophical approach to the agency's efforts on the client's behalf.

Research

Among the various traditional compensation methods by which clients have paid their agencies is one that provides for payment as a percentage of sales: the advertising works, sales increase, the agency is rewarded for its role. Simple.

In 1989, the Carnation Company, a unit of Nestle, announced a new type of compensation plan based on how advertising scored in research. Score high, you get more; low, you get less. With an ad budget of more than $60 million, the company utilized at least four agencies compensated on this basis. Carnation believed that sales were a function of many things, but research scores would indicate to what degree advertising was one of them.

The art of poll-taking had most definitely reached a new level of importance. "Good research leads to good advertising," Hank Seiden, CEO of Ketchum Advertising in New York, wrote in *Advertising Age*. "Don't settle for a general answer—demand a detailed description of the target audience. The better you know your customers, the better you can sell them."

Mr. Seiden's advice is out of Journalism 101. He says successful advertising begins by knowing *Who? What? How?*

Who are we talking to?
What do we say to them?
How do we say it?

The second and third questions are best addressed by the agency's creative department, but number one is all research.

David Ogilvy offers that "advertising people who ignore research are as dangerous as generals who ignore decades of enemy signals."

John O'Toole contends, "Research provides the stuff that ads are made of: information. Thus it is the most important function of all."

Research, it seems, has come a long way from the days when many ad directors dismissed it as "spending money to have people tell me what I already know." Worse, there have been times over the years that research was said to be the device or vehicle a marketing director used to avoid having to take responsibility for a decision.

With the tremendous growth, success, and prestige of many research organizations, such as Gallup, Nielson, Opinion Research Corp., Harvey, Starch and others, and common uses of the technological advances, the business of research has evolved into an industry itself. To many people, a Nielson rating or a Starch score carries power. Who could imagine election night without a new poll to review every two or three minutes?

Some agencies believe they offer something of an alternative to research: themselves. The contention is, after years of experience and successful campaigns, they *know* what kinds of advertising works. They *know* how to get the public to respond to an ad—who needs to spend money on research?

The answer is, almost everybody who wants to succeed. You may have heard the expression that knowledge is power. Some may get too much power; no one has ever had too much knowledge.

The question of who performs or supervises research isn't that complicated. If the agency has a research department, utilize it. If not, there are enough private research firms of varying capabilities and costs to make the process eminently manageable.

Exactly how much of your ad budget should be devoted to research depends on a number of considerations, at least one of which is how much you need to know. Keep in mind that your own opinion does not constitute research simply because you think you are right.

First, establish your foundation:

- Who is your audience?
- Who are your competitors?
- How well are you and/or your product known—alone and relative to your competition?
- Does your public recognize the benefits of your product?
- What media will you need to use to reach your audience effectively?
- What are the major problems with, objections to, and criticisms of your company or your product?
- How are you perceived overall?

If you are a member of a trade association, some research studies or surveys may be available to you at little or no cost through your association.

Once you have identified your audience, your ad agency should be able to acquire a reasonable amount of research data without cost from media sources. For example, if your target audience is senior management of large corporations, such media as *The Wall Street Journal, Business Week, Fortune, Forbes,* and *Barron's* will provide you with studies of varying levels of detail and sophistication. They want your ad business and will try to convince you that their readers are your target market. Should this prove true, they can and will gladly provide at least some information on the makeup of these individuals' stock portfolios, real estate holdings, vacations, hobbies, personal luxury items (owned or rented), favorite sports, club memberships, credit cards, and so on. Believing that any information available is useful, remember, this is also free. Be suspicious as to what extent they may have interpreted the data to favor their own publications or media.

If your budget permits, have your agency meet with consultants and research organizations to explore two options: privately commissioned research you might have conducted on your behalf and lower cost research in which you are a participant/co-sponsor with others in your profession with whom you then share the data.

Clients typically insist they know their audience—who their customers are and what they're looking for. And maybe they do. Ad agencies are frequently accused of telling clients what they want to hear. And sometimes they do. The most common error is to assume our audience shares our opinions and preferences—simply, agrees with us because our argument is correct.

Whether you believe you already know your market or your special talent lies in manipulating and interpreting data, research studies can usually be counted on to tell you something you didn't know.

*   *   *   *   *

One such study for a major financial services company slightly disappointed the client when it failed to uncover evidence of significant gains in awareness and customer satisfaction following a strong ad campaign. The *good* news was that the survey revealed nearly every one of their competitors ratings *declined* in those two categories during the same period.

*   *   *   *   *

It has been said that change is the only constant. To believe this is to recognize the value of continually taking the pulse of your market to follow such change: research.

Advertising typically looks at research as valuable at four stages in the process:

1   Defining the market
2   Defining the direction of creative work
3   Testing
4   Tracking

The first stage begins in the client's office with the agency asking for all information the client has regarding their market, competition, and customers—their preferences, prejudices, and attitudes.

- Who are your customers (men, women, children, white collar, blue collar, race, age, income, sex, ethnic influence, geographic influence, conservative, risk-tolerance level)?
- What do your customers think of you relative to your competition (better, worse, cheaper, more expensive, overpriced, high quality, good value, fashionable, unfashionable, the same as everybody else)?
- Do your customers appreciate the benefits of your product?
- Why do people buy your products?
- Why do they *not* buy your products?
- Do sales increase
   —seasonally?
   —when products are discounted?
   —when products are endorsed by VIPs?
   —when you advertise?
   —following a favorable news story?
   —with rebate offers?

- What is your customer's best source of information about your company and products?
  —media coverage (TV, magazine, newspapers, radio)
  —word-of-mouth
  —media advertising

To best construct a customer profile database, begin by asking people for information. Tap as many sources as you can and don't overlook the obvious: your own personnel and your mailbox. What kind of mail (and phone calls) do you receive from customers? Angry? Complementary? Grateful? What do your employees hear about your company or products from friends, business contacts, relatives, and acquaintances? What feedback do you get from field personnel (sales reps, wholesalers, delivery people)?

Surveys

The next step is more ambitious. Mail and/or telephone surveys of persons within your industry and your customers can be conducted quickly and relatively inexpensively. Use your own database of current and past customers or buy lists from any number of good services. Develop a questionnaire that can be completed verbally or in writing in about twelve minutes (beyond fifteen minutes, people's attention and willingness to respond seem to lessen). A very direct approach such as, "Your opinion is of critical importance to us," seems to work well—much better than "Please take a few moments to answer some questions."

Depending on your business, location surveys are manageable and useful. These might include personal or written solicitations at supermarkets, shopping malls, airports, public parks, theatre lobbies, commuter stations, and beaches, for example.

There are numerous published reports that might be used instead of, or in addition to, your own survey data. Beyond what may be available from trade associations, newsletters such as The Roper Organization's *The Public Pulse* are excellent sources of monitoring what the market is looking for in products and services and in reflecting attitudes. Its sister service, *Roper Reports*, has long been an invaluable vehicle for information. Publications like *American Demographics* take the approach of a monthly magazine. If your industry is the subject of an article, one issue can be worth hundreds of times the annual subscription price. If not, it is nonetheless an easy and helpful read, offering small bits of information from many of the major research firms in addition to feature-length articles.

In some respects, research today can be as easy as supermarket shopping. For instance, if you have defined your target market as Hispanic, Southeast Asian or another ethnic group, there are very detailed and inclusive books available on marketing to these groups. They include heavy doses of research data. Older Americans—senior citizens, retirees or the semi-retired—are the focus of Robert Menchin's *The Mature Market: A Strategic Marketing Guide to America's Fastest-Growing Population Segment*. It provides as much data on this group, their buying patterns, interests and desires, as a research study costing several thousand dollars of just a few years ago. Surprisingly, such useful, easily available works are often overlooked in favor of original material. Authors of this type of book have spent months, sometimes years, collecting, comparing and interpreting data. *This* research provides an excellent complement to your current surveys and studies.

Telephone surveys are relatively inexpensive and can be targeted to certain cities or certain neighborhoods. How well known is your name or your product in Los Angeles when compared to Florida or Washington? Do you need to devote more of your budget to one market over another?

*   *   *   *   *

An investment company was preparing to launch a national campaign to raise its level of recognition and to increase its market share. But before it could claim it *raised* its name recognition, it had to determine what that level was prior to the campaign's launch. Four regions of the country were targeted—Chicago, New York, Los Angeles and South Florida. A questionnaire was developed by the ad agency's account service and research people. The client was asked to review it and comment, add to or delete any information.

For the purposes of this example, we will call the client firm *Joe's Investment Company*. A sample of the survey form the callers used is reproduced here.

Market Research Survey

NAME_____

ADDRESS_____

CITY_____STATE_____ZIP CODE_____

TELEPHONE_____

Hello, my name is _____ and I'm with a national market research firm. We're doing a study on investment and financial planning. May I please speak to the head of your household?

1. Sir/Ma'am, which of the following publications have you read within the last three to six months? (READ) (CHECK)

    Business Week   *The New Yorker*
    Newsweek   *Fortune*
    Changing Times   *Financial World*
    New York Times   *Personal Investor*
    Sunday Magazine   *Barron's*
    The Wall Street Journal   *Forbes*
    U.S. News & World Report

2A. Do you subscribe to cable television?
    Yes Ask Q2B
    No Skip to Q3

2B. Do you watch either Financial News Network or the Cable News Network, or both, at least occasionally?
    Yes
    No

IF RESPONDENT DOESN'T READ AT LEAST ONE OF
THE MAGAZINES MENTIONED IN Q1 OR WATCH
CNN/FNN—TERMINATE.

3. In the last year have you purchased a financial prod-
    uct—C.D., mutual fund, bonds, stocks, options or fu-
    tures contract, etc.—worth, at least $1,000?
    Yes
    No (Terminate)

4. Was your annual household income, prior to taxes,
    over or under $40,000 in 1987?
    Over
    Under (Terminate)

5. Are you:
    Under 30 years of age
    31 to 40
    41 to 50
    51 to 60
    Over 60

6A. Which firms have you heard of which offer or spon-
    sor investment products or tax sheltered invest-
    ments? (RECORD BELOW)

	Q6A Unaided	Q6B Aided
National Investments	_____	_____
American Investments	_____	_____
United Investments	_____	_____
Inter-American Co.	_____	_____
Global Investors	_____	_____
Universal Investors	_____	_____
World-Wide Investors	_____	_____
Downtown Investors	_____	_____
Joe's Investment Co.	_____	_____

7. I'd like you to tell me which of the following sym-
    bols are associated with which investment company
    (ROTATE ORDER)

Symbols	Company
An Eagle	_____
A Horse	_____
A Light Bulb	_____
A Cloud	_____

8. Now I'd like you to tell me which of the following slogans are associated with which investment firm? (ROTATE ORDER)

Slogan	Company
"Invest with us"	_____
"Investing with a good attitude"	_____
"It's your money and we want it"	_____
"We earn our commission every day"	_____
"The financial future is here"	_____
"Get your share"	_____

IF CORRECT SYMBOL FOR JOE'S INVESTMENTS COMPANY NOT MENTIONED UNAIDED IN Q7 ASK Q9A FOR THOSE WHO EXPRESS EITHER AIDED OR UNAIDED AWARENESS OF JOE'S INVESTMENTS IN Q6. OTHERS SKIP TO Q11.

9. What is the symbol for Joe's Investments Company?

_____

IF CORRECT JOE'S LOGO NOT MENTIONED IN Q8, ASK Q9B FOR THOSE WHO EXPRESS EITHER AIDED OR UNAIDED AWARENESS IN Q6. OTHERS SKIP TO Q11.

9B. What is Joe's Investment Company's slogan?

_____

Now I'd like you to rate Joe's Investment Company on the following dimensions using five point scales. (RO-TATE SCALE POINTS. DON'T READ DON'T KNOW)

10A. Stability. Would you say they are:
      5. Extremely Stable
      4. Stable
      3. Neither Stable nor Unstable
      2. Unstable
      1. Extremely Unstable
      0. Don't Know

Why?_____

10B. Integrity. Would you say they are:
      5. Extremely Honest
      4. Honest
      3. Neither Honest nor Dishonest
      2. Dishonest
      1. Extremely Dishonest
      0. Don't Know

Why?_____

10C. Quality of Products. Would you say their financial products are:
      5. Excellent
      4. Good
      3. Fair
      2. Poor
      1. Very Poor
      0. Don't Know

Why?_____

10D. Service on financial products. Would you say they are:
      5. Excellent
      4. Good

    3. Fair
    2. Poor
    1. Very Poor
    0. Don't know

Why?_____

10E.   Value. Would you say the financial products they
       offer are:
       5. Excellent value for the money
       4. Good value for the money
       3. Fair value for the money
       2. Poor value for the money
       1. Very Poor value for the money
       0. Don't Know

Why?_____

11A.   Finally, have you seen, heard or read any
       advertising for Joe's Investment Company?
            Yes (Ask Q11B)
            No (Terminate)

11B.   Where was it (each one)? (RECORD BELOW)

11C.   Describe it (each)? (PROBE FOR COPY POINTS &
       GRAPHICS)–(RECORD BELOW)

11B	11C	
Media	*Description*	
	Graphics	*Copy*
Radio		
TV		
Magazine		
Direct Mail		
Billboard		
Newspaper		
Other_____		

(THANK HIM OR HER AND TERMINATE)

The success of the ad campaign isn't just a result of knowing your customer well, but in knowing *if* and *to what extent* your customer knows you.

This first stage, assembling the profile of your customer and your market, is the single most important research file you will create. There is no way your advertising can achieve maximum effectiveness without the very basic knowledge of what you are selling to whom and under what circumstances.

The second research stage begins after the agency has channeled all collected data into the creative process and created ads that speak to the identified target market in a manner that will get its attention and interest. It is the stage that asks "Did we do it? Are we on target?"

The route to testing the creative work may employ some of the same channels as the previous studies or surveys: the supermarket/shopping mall/airport/commuter station circuit. The same random subjects who told you what they cared about are now asked to tell you if you heard them correctly. How do they respond to the ads you've created? Will they buy the product?

Focus Groups

Probably the fastest growing form of ad testing is one that has been in use for a very long time: the focus group. As Thomas Greenbaum, creative Vice President of Clarion Marketing & Communications in Greenwich, Connecticut, wrote in *Advertising Age*: ". . . the 1980's saw the focus group industry mature to become the most widely used type of market research. The use of groups over the past ten years expanded from the package goods companies into financial services, hard goods and industrial applications."

Typically, the focus group is eight or nine people gathered around a conference table. These are people who have been chosen by the research team as being representative of the client's target audience. They are paid a modest fee for participating. A food tray is brought in and every attempt is made to make them as relaxed as possible. A professional moderator will lead the discussion, ask questions, and gently keep the proceedings on track.

Because focus groups have been around so long, it would be naive to believe participants don't know they are being both observed and recorded, always on audio and frequently on video tape. The ad agency's account team, as well as client representatives and research analysts, will be watching for subtle physical responses and facial gestures, as well as comments, to evaluate the group participants' responses. Upon being presented finished work or work in-development, the observers will want to look for initial reactions and comments and wait to determine if some people can articulate or support their opinions. Are they being influenced by other members of the group? Are they over-analyzing? Saying what they think the observers want to hear?

Are they playing to the camera?

Van Kampen Merritt, a successful investment banking and financial services firm, was presented with two campaigns, both built around its theme, "Investing with a sense of direction." (Two ads from this campaign are shown in another section of this book.) The agency was very comfortable with both campaigns. One was a very solid, straightforward depiction of the ad theme: a photograph of a lighthouse and a single word—*Direction*—above brief copy on charting an investment course. The second campaign was the same headline and copy, but instead of the photo, the lighthouse was illustrated from a distance across a dark, angry sea.

*   *   *   *   *

Focus groups were scheduled to see and hear how representative members of the client's target group reacted to the two campaigns. What follows is an excerpt from one of those sessions. (Note: the group in this excerpt has been edited. The eight-person group has been reduced to five, as some persons echoed the opinions of others):

Moderator: I am going to show you an ad and I'd like you to look at it for what it says to you overall and then I'd like some specifics, such as what do you think of the headline, the picture . . . the ad copy—is it too long or too short or interesting or dull or . . . what? I'd like to know what you think.

1st woman: I like the photograph. It's very pretty. There's not too much to read. It's short and to the point. I like that.

1st man: It's a nice ad—very clean, a lot of space around the picture. The word "Direction" and a picture of a lighthouse. That suggests safety to me, like you're going in the right direction.

2nd man: I like it. It's very subtle. I hate it when they try to beat you over the head with an ad. You know, about how wonderful they are and make a lot of promises. This just says 'a sense of direction' and shows a lighthouse. I like the simplicity of that.

1st woman: It's a very restful picture, but it says "strength" to me.

2nd woman: I'm not really sure how I feel about this. I guess I'd like to know more about the company, you know, like what they stand for and how successful they are at investing. This is a picture of a lighthouse, but what does it tell me about the company?

2nd man: It tells you their symbol is a lighthouse—

3rd man: She's got a point. I like a lot of information before I give my money to someone. This doesn't tell me too much about how they operate.

Moderator: Well, it says they're a division of Xerox. Does that say anything to you? And that they've "sponsored over $20 billion" of investments. What—

2nd man: I like that. They say they're part of Xerox and use a dollar figure to say they're big so they don't have to go on for two pages about how great they are. I don't read really long ads anyway. This gives me just enough.

1st woman: It does say to see your broker for more information—

2nd man: Yeah, well, I think they all have to say that, but this ad works for me—it gets my attention with the picture and the large white border. It kind of pops out . . .

Moderator: Okay, thanks. I'm going to take this ad down now. I'll put it back up in a few minutes. I'd like you to take a look at another ad. It's for the same company. Same headline, same text message. This time, though instead of a photograph, you see we have an artist's drawing of a dark and stormy sea and an illustrated lighthouse in the distance. It's casting its beam out across the sea to show "Direction" as the headline says. What do you think of this version?

2nd man: I like it. It's very arty. Very moody.

1st woman: I think it's kind of scary. It's too dark—

2nd woman: I agree. It's too dark. The first one made me feel very secure. I mean the picture suggested a more calm, secure situation. This is very unsettling.

3rd man: I think the lighthouse looks more like a house in some gothic scene. Very foreboding.

2nd man: I disagree. The ocean looks dark and angry. The lighthouse in the distance says safety . . . I think it's a very strong idea.

1st man: Well, you have to remember this ad is for a financial company. I don't know about this. If I'm going to be giving them my money, I'd like to be reassured. This has a very uneasy look about it.

2nd man: That's the point. It's a symbol, the angry ocean, the lighthouse is safety. The company's the lighthouse. The ocean is the stock market or whatever, rolling all over the place—

1st woman: The scene almost looks religious. You know, so dark and stormy and this ray of light in the distance—

2nd man: Beam of light.

Moderator: Okay. Let me put up the first ad again. With both of them side by side, let me ask you which you prefer, in terms of its attention-getting ability? Second, as investor, which ad might make you call your broker to find out more about what they have to offer?

     *   *   *   *   *

We'll put an end to the suspense: the ad with the photograph was preferred by three out of five. Our **2nd man** liked the angry sea version and another member of the group thought both versions were interesting in different ways and couldn't really decide between the two. On the more important question, however, of which ad might prompt a call to the broker, the choice was ad number one, by a rather interesting margin of 5-0. Even the fan of the second version said, in the final analysis, there was something "straightforward and traditional" in the way the first ad took him through the message and asked him to call.

An interesting phenomenon occurs sometime in surveys, interviews, and discussions—people lie. All people don't lie all the time (thus rendering the research not only inaccurate, but pointless), but it seems some people feel a need to impress, to say things they believe will get a particular reaction. For example, a television commercial using humor may elicit a smile (a desired response) only to have the viewer describe it as stupid—not funny at all. For whatever reason, the viewer felt embarrassed to admit enjoying (or at least responding) to something silly in the commercial. Other spots that use strong sexual overtones as an element may draw a response of cool indifference—even an exaggerated coolness—because it would appear immature to admit an appreciation for advertising that clearly utilizes sex as an exploitation device. Print and TV ads for Calvin Klein's "Obsession" and print ads for *Lear's* magazine are two examples of this. Both campaigns use powerful visuals of nude and seminude models, artfully photographed. Both campaigns have been extremely effective in generating awareness and recall. Yet there is a reluctance, almost an uneasiness, on the part of respondents to acknowledge any impact of the ads.

Sometimes, it's as simple as it seems. People answer honestly, their responses are logical, and a sensible dialogue ensues on what they liked and didn't like about the work. But there are times when the observers have to try to determine what the viewers mean when they say something that doesn't quite fall together with what's being experienced. If the process sounds complicated, it's one reason why researchers consider psychology such an important part of what they do.

If your focus group laughs at the jokes or compliments the footage of the sunset or the use of a classic Gershwin melody, that's good. But what you're looking for is: Does the work grab their attention? How much of what was said do they recall? Will they remember the product showcased? Was the message sufficiently strong and relevant that they will remember it later? Is there a motivation to buy? Or . . .

Did the music distract? Did the model seem like every model in every TV commercial? Was the material confusing or offensive? Or . . . just not very interesting?

We want the audience to love our commercials, but we *need* them to remember and be motivated to buy the product. Getting awards and having people ask their friends if they saw that beautiful TV spot for our product is very flattering, but it's not effective advertising if it doesn't ultimately result in a sale.

In a focus group viewing TV spots to sell Cable TV subscriptions, one participant noted, "It's not just *more* television, it *better* television." The line was later incorporated into the spot.

Listen. Watch. Evaluate. Note how people respond to the work. Then fine tune, based on the feedback you receive. If you question the group's responses, repeat the focus group tests again. Soft or contradictory responses could mean the spots don't work . . . or it could mean the group is inappropriate. Repeat the test with another group, if in doubt, before revising or spending thousands of dollars on media.

Focus groups are not foolproof. Sometimes groups respond well to a "rough" of an ad or spot and the finished work fizzles. An example of this was the Australian muscleman Jacko in a series of TV spots for Eveready batteries. The script, the concept and the storyboards won high marks in tests, but the campaign was ultimately remembered for being so awful. People loved to talk about it—to tell others how very unpleasant they thought it was.

And somebody at Burger King or its agency or research unit must have produced evidence that the "Where's Herb?" campaign would go on to become something other than one of advertising history's great embarrassments.

Testing is anything but foolproof, but, again, it attempts to provide advance information on how the work will be received before the major portion of the budget is committed to media. The work is used in a controlled and limited way, such as in a movie theatre, where crowd reaction will be instant and clear. Most movie audiences resent the intrusion of advertising on a movie screen.

Nonetheless, after the initial irritation of the presence of the commercial, the audience accepts that it's there and reacts. Coca Cola used spots with actress Demi Moore in a mini-movie boy-meets-girl humorous spot: Two minutes of movie-quality production values and a cute, brief story line. The audience response was highly positive. The same for spots featuring the Pointer Sisters and singer Kim Carnes in short, musical pieces. Shorter re-edited versions later aired on TV. Another test run might air in a selected market during a highly rated show with phone follow-up the next day. If the researcher can locate a number of people who watched the show (not too difficult) they are questioned as to any details they might recall about the spot. This is obviously regarded by many as better than *no* research, but still of the "shot-in-the-dark" school.

Some in-theatre tests are by invitation only: a group is invited to view and rate new television program pilots. While there, they are also asked to view and comment on new TV spots. Sometimes both the shows and the commercials are in rough form. The audience not only doesn't object, but usually likes the novelty of seeing work-in-progress. They then go on to view the work much more critically and their responses must be evaluated for legitimacy.

The *tracking* stage of the research, very simply, tells you if what you've created has worked—or not. It's a good idea to have pre-campaign data to help you more clearly define your own results. That is, you can't claim the new ad campaign has increased awareness by 15 percent if you didn't know the level of awareness before the campaign began running. So stage one of tracking results means logging your initial data, against which your results will be measured. This exercise forces you to set goals and objectives.

By posting your pre-campaign information and charting your progress, you must also allow for flexibility in your marketing and media plan. For example, don't order media for the calendar year if you are going to track your effectiveness at four-or six-month intervals.

Those intervals are when fine-tuning of your plan should be done.

Does research guarantee success?

Of course not. A classic example was the ABC-TV morning news program *A.M. America*. It was virtually invented by market research. The colors of the set (blue, orange and yellow), the bouncy synthesizer theme music, the perfect age/skin color/profile Barbie and Ken co-hosts, the features—everything market research said the public wanted in a morning television show. It was not only promoted for its hosts and features, but for the fact that it was the result of careful surveys and analysis to develop the perfect show.

It was an immediate disaster.

The set looked great. The music was bouncy. The hosts were attractive and professional. But the whole program had the look and feel of having been put together by a computer instead of a production team. The human touch was noticeably missing. When someone is praised as having a feeling for what works, it is usually a base of data of what the market wants and the talent to address that image.

U.S. News & World Report ran a story wherein a researcher monitored a group of consumers' purchases for a year and concluded that television advertising had almost no effect on their buying habits. While even the most ardent of TV bashers might want to embrace that conclusion, it was hard to swallow. The article noted that ". . . people aren't always completely honest when asked what they like about an ad or product. If asked directly why they bought a particular car, for example, people reply that it handles well or is dependable, but not that driving it makes them feel like James Bond or an oil tycoon."

"Making them feel like James Bond" touches on an extremely important component of the advertising effort that will be more obvious in the creative stage of the process. That component is the psychological element. To what *degree* people identify with the people they see in ads is a highly elusive conclusion and will vary with each individual. *That* they identify is an accepted truth. The models in the health club ads, the Marlboro man, women in hair care and perfume ads—even the celebrity endorsers, from movie stars to athletes—represent the people the targets of the ads aspire to be. The unspoken phrase is, "This can be you if you use this product." Buy the clothes, buy the car, wear the fragrance . . . and all your dreams will come true. It is important to know *why* people buy. Ad dollars are wasted if the advertising focuses on quality and value when . . . the customer's only concern is that it smells good. Ads won't succeed if we sell to vanity while the customer's concern is safety.

Make your research answer the *why* questions.

Research studies allow you to get a handle on your competition. Sales figures will tell you *what* they're doing and *how* they are doing it will be easy enough to spot. Answering the *why* question may teach you something. Why are they running ads in *Sassy* while yours are in *Time* and *Fortune*? Why are their commercials on daytime TV dramas and game shows, while you're on the weekend news? Your competitive analysis is a way to tap into someone else's research. If they are doing something differently and it seems to be working, look below the surface and analyze how they reached their conclusions.

Consider, too, the impact your ads have on satisfied customers. They tend to make them *more* satisfied. Once a customer has made a major purchase, he or she wants to be reassured of the correctness of the decision. That is the reason for such classic ad phrases as "Four out of five smokers recommend_____" or "More than a million copies sold." The reaffirmation of a smart decision makes the customer feel good . . . and recommend the product to others . . . and buy again.

Merchandising the results of positive research is another use for the information and another sales opportunity.

In our survey questionnaire (for Joe's Investment Company) and our focus group (for Van Kampen Merritt) we used examples in the financial services field. Perhaps we learned something in that research about a particular preference for the product among older persons living in Florida. Sharing that information with that audience allows another sales option: an ad, a mailing, a radio or TV spot or billboard—perhaps a newsletter—that announces, "The choice of South Florida seniors." When research turns up some surprising good news, use it.

We fashion images for ourselves. We are influenced by what we see. We see a lot of advertising. Understand it and make it work for you.

In Review

For your advertising to succeed, you need to know your market—your customer, your competition and all the factors that affect both.

1   *Define your market.* Know who you are talking to in terms of age, sex, marital/family status, business/profession, income/geographic influence.

2   *Identify your competition.* This includes both direct and indirect competitors. Be realistic, but consider that such businesses as restaurants, bowling alleys, video stores and movie theatres are all competing for the leisure time and budget. It's not only restaurant verses restaurant.

3   *Prepare a competitive analysis.*

4   *Determine how much your customer knows about your company and product, alone and relative to your competition.* Older, younger, cheaper, more costly, better, not as good—know how you are perceived overall.

5   *Identify your customers main sources of information about your products.* Media coverage, advertising, word of mouth.

6 *Know why your business grows better or worse.* Seasonality, discounts/rebates, advertising, news coverage, endorsements.

7 *Know what you want your advertising to accomplish.* Increase awareness, reverse a negative image or rating, increase sales, expand markets.

8 *Merchandise your research.* Use the data collected to tell you things you need to know (the who, what, why and how) and then re-use it to exploit positive conclusions as sales opportunities.

9 *Establish benchmarks for results.* You know where you've been. You know where you're going. Establish how far and how fast and adjust your plan along the way.

Planning

Today, different businesses, like different countries, have their own languages. Check the bookshelves and you will find *The Language of Wall Street* or *The Language of Finance*. And everywhere, of course, is that most rapidly growing of all forms of communication, computers. In advertising, it is not the quirky terms (ADIs, CPMs, voice-overs, narrowcasting, layouts, and mechanicals) that are at issue here, but what we truly understand a certain term to mean.

For example, an account supervisor told an account executive that they were lacking a media plan.

"Here it is," the AE offered, pushing a page across the desk.

"No, that's a media *schedule*, not a media *plan*," the supervisor corrected, to a blank-faced response.

The account exec thought that the list of media, with dates, times, frequency, and costs was a plan, and had been allowed to continue thinking so for many years. The media *plan* considered the strategy, the objectives and, most importantly, a rationale for why certain media were recommended over others.

That's a problem magnified with regard to a *marketing plan*. It is assumed or defined as so many different things.

The marketing plan is basically a scheme of how the product or service will be priced, distributed and promoted.

Today's very trendy term *integrated marketing* really deals more with the promotional aspects of marketing, using public relations, sales promotion, and advertising, than it does with fundamental marketing as it relates to pricing, distribution or actual selling.

The marketing plan tells us: *what* we are going to do and *how* we are going to do it.

Within the marketing plan lies the *strategy*. Typically, the strategy addresses a clearly defined *objective*.

Les Bogart, in his book *Strategy in Advertising*, notes correctly a principal flaw in most advertising strategies: they are developed from the perspective of the seller. After all, ad agencies are working for the seller.

"Implicit in the mind of the advertising planner," Mr. Bogart writes, "is the notion of an audience of consumers, real or potential, with varying degrees of propensity for using his product, frequently or in substantial quantities, and in various stages of predisposition to buy it."

While Mr. Bogart may have a tendency to get a bit wordy, the point is valid. When devising a strategy, take care that you don't make sweeping assumptions, particularly when your research has told you there is a market for your product and helped you identify an audience that needs and wants your product. If you assume that all you have to do is show the product and wait for the sales to roll in, you'll be disappointed.

". . . the real function of advertising looks very different when seen from the standpoint of the *buyer* rather than the seller," Mr. Bogart notes.

The prospective buyer of a product has likely not tuned in a TV or radio program for your commercial, nor purchased a magazine or newspaper for your ad. Your presence as an advertiser is something to be endured in exchange for the information and entertainment value of the media.

Advertising, particularly broadcast advertising, is intrusive and almost always resented. And so much of it is regarded as, simply, bad.

So your strategy, which may have had as its objective to increase brand awareness and raise sales levels, must at least to some extent devote part of the plan to overcoming a predisposition against advertising.

Yes, the consumer is going to buy a product. But why *your* product?

Walt Disney built an empire around the philosophy that everything produced, from a Mickey Mouse cartoon to a nature program to a musical comedy, should both educate and entertain.

The best advertising educates and entertains. Maybe the extent of the education is only why your brand has greater benefits than that of your competitor. The consumer wants to know, "What's in it for me? Why should I care about your product?" You've intruded on their time and space. You're unwelcome. Make them like you.

Benefits. That's why they will care.

Entertainment is the reason they will read the ad and watch and listen and remember the commercials. More than once.

If your objective is to move product and increase your market share—the objective of nearly every company—give the public what it wants: information, entertainment and value—in terms of price and other benefits.

The Agency/Client Partnership—Who Does What

This section may prove to be somewhat controversial. It is intended to be candid and useful. Some people's feelings may get hurt. It has much to do with separating our own tastes from what others like. The presumption is that few advertising agencies will ever tell clients that they are *bad* clients. That presumption is probably somewhere between reasonably and absolutely correct.

Agencies might make gentle references to "unreasonable expectations," but will not come right out and say to a client that the client is bad. The reason is obvious. If the statement is offered, it tends to be an unfinished thought, as in ". . . so we can no longer work for you." Or ". . . and if you don't shape up, we're walking." Odds are that the client would respond with "Well, don't let the door hit you on your way out." No research suggests clients might respond with "We're sorry. We'll try to do better in the future."

Managers of ad agencies work hard to land accounts in an increasingly competitive environment of shrinking budgets and odd compensation deals. And they have overhead—rent, expenses, staff salaries. For this reason, they normally take a deep breath and swallow hard before saying, "We'll give you whatever you want," instead of, "We'll give you what we believe you need to succeed."

If you truly want to get the best and the most from your agency, examine to what degree you or your associates are helping or hindering the effort.

"Whose ad is it anyway?"

"Whose ad is it anyway?"—this plaintive cry echoes as the client tries to suggest a change in the ad. Not a very *big* change—just perhaps a word or two . . . maybe a color . . . an illustration . . . a headline . . . and, of course, this 900-word disclaimer that legal wants . . . in a box . . . at the top of the ad. Minor stuff, really. Revisions by tomorrow noon?

The truly core issue of the working relationship between agency and client—the real point in getting the best and the most from your agency—is defining *who does what.*

Earlier we described lawyers and ad agencies as natural enemies. Some days it may seem as if ad agencies and their clients, perhaps, are the *real* natural enemies.

Consider: a client holds an agency review. The agency makes it from the long list (of twelve) to the short list (of five) to become a finalist (one of three). Finally, after absorbing an entire deodorant stick in what seems like minutes, the selection is made. Hands are shook. Champagne is opened. The client has selected an agency based on months of evaluating and eliminating. The agency chosen was called "outstanding," with dynamite creative, solid research, and as sharp a team of media and account service people as has ever been assembled at one address. Why, then, does it seem to the agency people as if, from the moment the champagne bubbles stop bubbling, the client won't step back and let them do their job?

It has always been thus.

Ad agencies want to create good ads to hang on their walls, to win awards, and to use in attracting new business. Art directors, copywriters, and creative directors want to include these ads in their portfolios. So if everyone wants to create good ads, why is there so much really bad advertising?

According to understandably off-the-record opinions of the agency people, the simplest answer is *clients.*

Their theory (complaint? lament?) is that advertisers are mostly responsible for much of the bad advertising we see. That statement should not be expected to win a lot of friends among ad managers and directors—no one appreciates being attacked. The point of this work, however, is not to say to clients hoping to get the most from their ad agencies "Great job! Keep it up! Kick back and relax. You're doing fine."

The point is to get the best that you can. That means that if you *don't* believe you are getting the best, some changes may be in order. A new agency or some major overhauling of your present agency may be needed. But some major changes in *how you operate* may be in order as well.

The new head of marketing for a major financial institution called in his ad agency and said he was planning to replace them. He said he wanted a new direction. The agency people responded that they were in the third year of a highly successful, award-winning campaign. The marketing chief said he didn't much like the campaign anyway.

"I'm no expert on advertising," he announced, "but I know what I like."

His idea was to replace a campaign that used rich, lush photographs, bold headlines, and a call to action with "a puzzle or a contest or something like that."

The agency lost the battle . . . and the account. The new agency tried a couple of approaches (not puzzles or contests) during the remainder of the marketing chief's brief tenure. Ultimately, the client went back to using some of the original ads.

Corporate CEO Harvey Mackay, in his bestselling book *Beware the Naked Man Who Offers You His Shirt*, devotes several pages to the subject of advertising in a chapter titled "Why Your Ads Don't Work." He asks the question: "What's the difference between good advertising and bad advertising?" His answer: "More often than not, it's good clients and bad clients. Unfortunately, advertising is one of those soft sciences in which everyone regards himself as an expert. The results often are ads that are designed for a target audience of one, the guy who pays the bills. Agencies will offer opinions, but there aren't many who are going to refuse a client who insists on having his own way . . ."

Mr. Mackay's advice is transmitted in nine rules for better advertising. We offer here excerpts from four of them.

Rule 1: *Stay out of the picture.* For every Lee Iacocca, there are 1,001 jerks who insist on having their own faces leering out . . . because "the public knows me" or "the agency wants me to."

Rule 2: *Don't be your own copywriter.* This is a common failing of intelligent people, particularly lawyers and CEOs (the kind who write lots of memos) . . . intelligent people like this dismiss the efforts of professional copywriters as too flashy and commercial. They want to "educate" the public. Mostly they want to say what they want to say the way they want to say it . . . If the body copy gets read, it's a miracle.

Rule 3:   *Disband the advertising committee.* Hire an advertising manager . . . There's no safety in numbers.

Rule 4:   *Don't play it safe.* . . . It just isn't interesting enough to be noticed.

The concluding thought in Mr. MacKay's dissertation is worth repeating (often): "Think of it as hiring an employee who is in charge of installing and maintaining the most complicated piece of machinery in your shop. Tell him where the switch box is and if the machine is doing what it's supposed to, but don't tell him how to do his job."

To a large extent this is attempting to change human nature. Few professions offer an individual a position without someone to whom he or she must report. In many instances the supervised can be heard lamenting of the supervisor: "I wish he (she) would just back off and let me do my job." This is more true of advertising than most businesses because advertising is so much a part of *everyone's* life, every day. We cannot help but be exposed to it on TV, radio, billboards, trains, planes, and bus stations, and our own daily mail. So advertising, like the postal service, the death penalty, Richard Nixon, and foreign aid, is something about which most everybody has a strong opinion. Unfortunately for those in the profession, it is a field, as Mr. Mackay notes, where "everyone regards himself as an expert."

The fact is that in advertising everyone pretty much *is* an expert. From the old curmudgeon (doubting the claims of faster, better, cheaper, and more powerful in TV commercials for everything from laxatives to snowblowers) to the child (doubting the claims of faster, better, cheaper, and more powerful for everything from beebee guns to skateboards).

We all know what we like.

We all know about the things to which we respond positively and negatively.

When people look at a TV commercial and say, "That stinks," or look at a magazine spread and say, "This is a terrible ad," they mean it. And their opinions are just as valid as the opinions of the people who created the ads.

The trade weekly *Advertising Age* publishes a section with letters sent to the publication. In nearly every issue, readers submit their candidates for "Ads We Can Live Without." In most cases these ads show buxom female models in bikinis or less, being used to sell tractors, printing supplies, even fire arms. These ads and others that use crude humor or sexism offend much of the audience—male and female.

Increasingly, because of the rise in drug abuse, alcoholism, teen pregnancies, suicides, and other social crises, advertisers have had to be much more sensitive in the messages they present. Once-funny lovable drunks aren't funny anymore. Advertisers are criticized for showing models smoking, drinking, or looking sexy.

So if anyone can qualify as an advertising "expert," what's the problem?

It is that everyone is not an expert when it comes to *creating* advertising.

David Ogilvy, in *Ogilvy on Advertising*, asserts "the wrong advertising can actually *reduce* the sales of a product . . . I sometimes wonder if there is a tacit conspiracy among clients, media, and agencies . . . Everyone involved has a vested interest in prolonging the myth that *all* advertising increases sales to some degree. It doesn't."

The challenge is to make *good* advertising. Creative people are credited with coming up with great ideas, great concepts. And they do. But the creativity in the most effective ads is in the *execution* of the good ideas. The *acceptance* of the ad's message by the audience has everything to do with their believing there is value in the message, a benefit to them—a reason for them to buy the product.

Jingles, jokes, and graphics will help people *remember* the product, but they don't provide a reason to buy.

The *reason to buy* may be translated as a benefit statement or, in "adspeak," it may be all or part of the *Unique
Selling Proposition* (USP). Call it what you will, you must
know not only what it *is*, but also how your target audience feels about it—alone and relative to your competition.

Do they think about it at all?

Should they?

Do they understand the relevance of what you bring
to their lives?

Do they even know you and/or your product exist?

Your research should have answered many of these
questions. Once you have the information, what are you
going to do with it? This is where both the creative process and the "how-to" part of the process begins. During
the stage of agency selection you were exposed to examples of the agency's creative talent. How that talent can
be put to work for you and how it interrelates with the
servicing of your account will define your relationship
with your agency.

In this work the word "client" is used instead of "advertiser" for two reasons. One is that "client" is a respectful term used in the trade to describe one side of the advertising relationship. We speak of agency/client relationships, not agency/advertiser relationships. The second
reason is that whoever is the contact on the client side is
the "client," whereas that person is the "advertiser" only
sometimes and rarely by definition. That is to say that the
real "advertiser" is the company or business, while the
contact person (client) may be the marketing director, advertising manager, vice president of communications,
senior vice president for corporate information, or any of
a hundred other individuals. An agency person would
comfortably introduce or refer to the holder of any of
those titles as "my client," never as "my advertiser." The
only time the client and the advertiser are one and the
same person is when he or she is in fact the owner of the
company *and* the contact person. In any case, to refer to

your client as your advertiser is, as a form of reference or address, awkward.

The reason for this exercise in designation is that the position of the person on the client side—his or her title, function, and area of expertise—is the major consideration in determining who does what in the relationship.

Note some of the more opinionated references offered earlier, such as Harvey MacKay's admonishment, "Don't be your own copy writer." An agency account person or copywriter will rarely be uncomfortable with a client offering copy changes or suggestions if the client happens also to be a writer. When the client's sales manager, chief financial officer, or lawyer rewrites the copy it becomes not only insulting to the writer, but usually somewhere between bad and totally unreadable. Offering glib remarks downplaying such situations as not really meaning to attack a copywriter's pride of authorship are misplaced. Your copywriter is a *professional author* and is expected to be proud of his or her work. That is why the writer is in that business. It is what the client is paying for. Agency copywriters don't pretend to have superior knowledge of law, yet lawyers routinely exceed the limits of their responsibility in advertising, adding excess verbiage that, under the guise of protection and clarification, frequently insults and confuses the audience for the ad.

The client CEO or other ranking official may be the world's best salesman, inventor, innovator, scientist, visionary, analyst, or deep-thinker. But when it comes to advertising, there is a sudden tendency for these otherwise bright people to feel they are writers, artists, or actors.

One reason is *control.* The fact that they control the ad space offers a highly seductive, ego-baiting opportunity to take center stage, not just take charge. Being in control of ad space offers a chance to live out a fantasy for many: a chance to speak to thousands—even millions—of people.

Writing seems easy. Everyone grew up writing letters, essays, and term papers, perhaps even a thesis or a dissertation. Armed with this background and the ultimate authority to decide "what runs," it is a great temptation to announce, "I know what I want it to say, I'll write it myself." Or, "This will have more credibility if I appear in the ad myself and seem to be talking directly to my customers." Or, "Let's do something fast and loud and bold—with an MTV kind of energy!"

Let go.

A first-rate administrator, whether of an advertising division or the entire company, doesn't need to become—or pretend to be—an advertising expert. You pay advertising experts to do that.

Further, consider the quality of your counsel. Don't frustrate your agency people by rejecting their media or strategy recommendations while heeding the counsel of your golf partners, family, and friends.

Too frequently clients will say "My wife thinks we should be in _____magazine. She reads it every week," or "Perkins in accounting had a great idea. I think we should try it."

It is correct—even terrific—to get comments from a diversity of sources, but Perkins in accounting or your wife (or husband) should not have more influence over your advertising than that given to your ad agency. If the day comes that you find yourself saying "My kids are coming up with better ideas than my agency," maybe you should be looking for a new agency. However, consider that you may very well have *positioned* yourself and your agency in such a way that you are more receptive to other influences, thus making the agency's job more difficult—maybe even impossible.

A sad fact of advertising is that many clients do not read the research reports or analysis or the recommendations of the agencies or even pay much attention in the meetings.

Why?

Usually, it's because the top people at most companies are conditioned to listen closely to their financial advisers, legal advisers and, frequently, outside consultants, and their close relatives and friends, and *The Wall Street Journal* and *Cable News Network*. But advertising is something that so many people believe they know and understand so well, that they only *half listen* (or wait to talk) or, worse, delegate the role of listener to someone who will give them a filtered, interpreted version of the message.

Of course there are the exceptions. Of the thousands of companies and businesses advertising today, the fact that the *largest companies are the largest advertisers is not a coincidence*. It is not simply because they are the ones with the money to advertise big. It is that they are the ones who recognize the *value* of advertising, invest heavily in knowing all aspects of the market, and invite the most innovative creative ideas. The fact that the fast-food chains, soft drink companies, and auto makers have both the most and the most *memorable* TV commercials in prime time is not an accident of programming.

Too often this frustrating scene is repeated. Senior management people return from a conference or trade association meeting, howling at what the competition is doing or planning—magazine inserts, tournament sponsorships, premiums, endorsements, and a celebrity spokesperson. "Why aren't *we* doing things like that?" the brass wants to know? The situation is frustrating because such ideas have probably already been recommended, only to be stalled or dismissed. Why? Because someone didn't understand them? Didn't agree with the research? Didn't want to spend the money that way? For any number of reasons, top management is having second thoughts about what the ad agency is doing for them.

We began by saying this material is intended for the person who has responsibility for advertising decisions and how important it is that person *believe in advertising*, its benefits and value.

Too often, the person in charge of advertising doesn't really have or chooses not to exercise the authority to implement decisions. This is a "corporate flaw" that the ad agency can't correct. If a marketing director or advertising manager has responsibility for the ad budget and the agency relationship, but can't approve a media schedule or a copy change without going back to a committee or, worse, layers of management, the client can never hope to achieve the maximum benefit of an advertising program. We cannot preach that a client should not be afraid to take risks when we can't get beyond the layers of approval stages.

So at the very top of the relationship we must establish that the client, having made a commitment to advertise and to support the effort to make that advertising the best and most effective it can be:

1   Will put someone in charge of advertising who has top management support and confidence, as well as authority to approve creative and media;

2   Will be available to provide information that assures the advertising is reflective of the client's character, goals and objectives;

3   Will listen and review presentations, with a solemn promise to praise or scowl, but let the ad director and the agency know if they're on track or not;

4   Will communicate concerns promptly should a problem arise, rather than letting irritations fester until the relationship grows tense.

Few people truly believe they are not creative, despite assertions to that effect. We often hear people say "I'm not a writer, but here's what I want the ad to say," or, "I'm not an artist, but I think a gold background with blue lettering and, maybe, some bullet points down the left side . . ."

Strike an understanding from the beginning that everyone's role is important, but everyone's role is not creative . . . and shouldn't be.

Here is a plan for structuring a productive working relationship. It works well with clients and agencies of most sizes, if they allow it.

The client designates the agency contact person, whether it be an ad manager or marketing V.P. If this person is not a part of the client's top management structure, someone from top management, ideally the chairman or president, agrees to meet with the agency's senior management every six months. Quarterly is better, but six-month intervals seem to work. A Christmas or New Year breakfast, lunch, or dinner meeting is a nice way to review, reflect, and look ahead.

The agency designates *its* point person. Depending on the size of the account and of the agency, this could be an account executive and/or an account supervisor.

A meeting should be arranged, to be held in the client's conference room, where everyone who will be involved in the management of the client's advertising can meet face to face. The agency team should include the account supervisor, account executive, creative director, art director, copywriter, and key assistants, if any. The client should present its team, which will have approval and implementation authority. The whole group shouldn't number more than ten. Remember, this is the *top tier* of management; if there are a dozen or more the account is doomed from the start. (The old analogy of too many cooks spoiling the soup originally could have been dreamed up to describe the dangers of too many people being involved in an ad agency/client relationship.)

The initial meeting is largely for introductions and exposition. The client contact and agency account exec will be day-to-day point people. The *client* team should present a detailed summary of:

1   The marketing/advertising goals and objectives as everyone understands them, *so* that everyone understands them;

2   Any and all available research;

3   Stories and anecdotes about the greatest successes of the previous agency's work on the account, the biggest disasters, why they occurred and what, if anything, was learned from the experience;

4   In round table form, everyone on the client's team should tell what they personally feel are the major strengths and weaknesses that will weigh on the ad program.

The agency team should present little or nothing. This meeting is convened because it is important to have a sense of the people who will be producing and receiving your work. The agency, at this stage, should be listening closely and learning as much as it can about the history, people, and qualities of the client it must now represent in the marketplace.

At this point, a determination can probably be made if any additional research is needed.

The agency team should get a short tour of the client's facilities. Often this helps familiarize the team with the tone of the client's operation. Though a company's plant or factory or studio or corporate headquarters may be of passing interest, it is largely irrelevant to its advertising. Advertising works when it shows the product or service in such a way that the public sees the benefits and responds. Such claims as "Second largest factory in California," or "Three million employees—and growing" flatter a client by focusing on them, but they are not of benefit to customers.

Following this first group meeting, the agency team should meet back at their own offices to review what they have seen and heard, measure it in relation to what they already know (having done their homework while working on landing the account) and what they still need to know. The account exec should be taking a lot of notes at this meeting because at 90 percent of future client meetings he or she will be meeting alone with the client contact. This is critical.

From this meeting comes the germ of a creative campaign or orders to go out and catch that germ. Perhaps an idea you developed for your spec creative presentation is the one you want to stay with, build, adapt, fine-tune; perhaps not. This is, however, the *next* big starting point in making good advertising.

What Makes a Good Ad?

Mal MacDougall of Jordan, McGrath, Case & Taylor answers, "Advertising isn't worth a damn if it doesn't excite customers."

John O'Toole, former chairman of Foote, Cone & Belding insists that "between strategy and execution there be a stage of development devoted totally to finding that *idea*."

"Nobody wants to be sold things," says Marty Weiss of Chiat/Day. "Everybody has got enough stuff. It's got to be something different."

Finally, David Ogilvy (usually considered the industry's final authority on weighty issues), writing in the classic *Confessions of an Advertising Man* in 1963: "a good advertisement is one which sells the product without drawing attention to itself."

A big idea.

A *breakthrough* (the 1980s short-form of the phrase, "breakthrough the clutter," meaning to stand out from the mass of advertising to which the public is exposed).

Something different.

Sells . . . without calling attention to itself.

To these we would add *offers a unique selling proposition*, a benefit to the consumer, a reason to buy.

If we understand anything at all about human nature, it is that people have a deep and abiding interest in themselves. Sell the benefits of the product *for* them *to* them and you've sold the product.

In an editorial on agency compensation, *Advertising Age* called attention to a point raised by some clients who felt that ad agencies were making too much money. For the most part, the agencies disagreed. *Ad Age*, however, made the point of asking, How much is too much? Rather, what is the "Big Idea" worth?

Their answer: "Millions, even billions of dollars to the fortunate client."

The magazine went on to list some examples of the "Big Idea":

- The Marlboro Man
- Does she or doesn't she? [Clairol]
- Don't leave home without it. [American Express]
- We try harder. [Avis]
- Melts in your mouth, not in your hand. [M&Ms]

Creativity is a highly subjective matter, but when an ad or a commercial can cause people to think of a product or company—and remember it—without even hearing its name, it is not only a creative "big idea," it is very good advertising.

What form should your work take? The very word "creative" implies the page is blank and opportunities are boundless. Expressions like "Dare to be different" address the point. The idea and approach can be as fresh as capabilities allow, so . . .

- Be honest
- Be believable
- Be different, go against trends
- Be positive
- Trust your instincts
- Educate, sell the benefits
- Entertain, be memorable
- Play by the rules

- Break the rules

That is to say, as in everything else, treat your business (creating advertising) *as* a business and approach it with maturity, professionalism, and respect. Don't insult your audience. Don't insult your competitors. Don't exceed the bounds of credibility or good taste.

While keeping all this in mind, be irreverent. Be dramatic. Be bold. Above all, be smart. Do your homework—about your audience and your competition. Good ideas come from a core of knowledge.

Just as, at the completion of the agency selection stage, the ad manager or director introduced the winning agency, the ad manager should be the first to see the idea and recognize its value. Then the idea is developed—copy, art, photography, presentation recommendations—and is presented to the senior client's management *by the agency*, with the ad director or manager introducing the presentation. This is an important point. Often the ad manager insists on presenting the work, sometimes without the agency account people even being present. This is never a good idea. The team that created the work deserves to present their ideas and experience the reaction, good or bad. They need either the reassurance that the client is behind the advertising or they need to sense the opposite firsthand. The agency team is also best equipped to field questions about the campaign. What was considered and rejected? Why?

But what if the ad manager, upon seeing the agency's creative, doesn't like it? Or hates it!

There are a couple of options: Test it. You don't need to call in the research firm just yet, but you can collect two or three groups of persons with known dissimilarities to view the work and offer an opinion. If enough of these people see something in the work, things missed by the ad manager, maybe the manager should concede that, while he or she may not like it, it still might be the right thing to do.

Everybody hates this approach.

The agency, believing in its idea, says, "Trust us. This is good stuff."

The ad manager says, "Maybe it is and maybe it isn't. Either way, I think it's the wrong approach."

While each party hates to lose a vote and *advertising by consensus* seems like an insulting method and a cop-out, it does have value. We use research to help us learn those things to which people respond favorably. If we disregard what others tell us because it's not what we want to hear or doesn't confirm our own tastes, we are letting arrogance guide our creative policy. That is worse than advertising by consensus.

Assuming the agency really believes in its recommendation, another course is to let them present it and an alternate idea. Agencies generally hate this approach too, and for the same reasons, but it is fair and reasonable. Just as some people love jazz or rock music while others hate it, responses to creative advertising are extremely subjective. If an agency is going to ask a client to "trust them" it should be on the basis of research and *knowledge*, not just a *sense* of how the work will perform.

If a client is going to bring in a talented group of professionals, the client must both expect and demonstrate professionalism and give them a chance to take their best shot. Creative people often indulge in screaming, swearing, and table-pounding. For better or worse, strong personalities sometimes behave that way. Usually a peaceful settlement is reached. The thing that should *not* be permitted is long explanations of what the advertising is supposed to do. When a TV spot or a magazine or newspaper ad runs, we don't have the luxury of a "set-up" to tell the audience what the following advertisement seeks to convey. If they don't get it when they see it, it isn't working and no amount of explaining that they are missing the point is going to help.

Clearly, if the relationship over the long term is a series of meetings and presentations from which both sides leave disappointed, there is an important question to address: is the chemistry wrong enough that agency and client should part company, or is one side or the other out of step with what the market needs and wants?

You might want to use the following list as a test or even a game—but creating these lines was more than a game to the companies that benefited from them. Some were slogans, some were ad headlines.

The $6 Billion List

Company	Slogan
AT&T	Let your fingers do the walking
AT&T	Long distance. The next best thing to being there.
Allstate Insurance	You're in good hands with Allstate.
Allied Van Lines	We move families, not just furniture
Ajax Cleanser	Ajax cleans like a white tornado.
Ajax Laundry Detergent	Stronger than dirt.
Ajax Cleanser	Ajax . . . the foaming cleanser
Alka Seltzer	Mama mia, that's a spicy meatball!
Alka Seltzer	Try it . . . You'll like it.
Alka Seltzer	I can't believe I ate the whole thing!
Alka Seltzer	plop, plop, fizz, fizz,—oh what a relief it is
American Express	Membership has its priveleges.
American Express	Do you know me? [famous names, not faces]
American Express	Don't leave home without it.
Armour Star Hot Dogs	The dogs kids love to bite.
Arpege Perfume	Promise her anything, but give her Arpege.

Aqua Velva	There's something about an Aqua Velva man.
Avis Rent-a-Car	When you're number 2, you've got to try harder.
Bic lighters	Flick your bic.
Brylcreem	A little dab'll do 'ya.
Bell System	Reach out and touch someone.
Budweiser	This Bud's for you.
Budweiser	Where there's life, there's Bud.
Bounty Paper Towels	The quicker picker upper.
Burger King	Home of the Whopper.
Burger King	Have it your way.
Breck shampoo	For stop 'n' stare hair.
Bayer Aspirin	Bayer works wonders.
Blackglama minks	What becomes a legend most?
Borden Dairy	If it's Borden's, it's got to be good.
Buick	Wouldn't you really rather have a Buick?
Buick	The great American road belongs to Buick?
Camel cigarettes	I'd walk a mile for a Camel.
Charmin tissue	Squeezably soft.
Charmin tissue	Don't squeeze the Charmin.
Carter's Infantwear	If they could just stay little until their Carter's wear out.
Chevrolet	See the USA in your Chevrolet.
Chevrolet	The heartbeat of America.
Clairol hair color	Does she or doesn't she? Only her hairdresser knows for sure.
Clairol Nice 'n Easy	The closer he gets, the better you look.
Clairol	Is it true blondes have more fun?
Chrysler	If you can find a better car, buy it.
Carnation	Milk from contented cows.
Continental Airlines	The proud bird with the golden tail.
Campbell Soups	Mmm Mmm good!
Curad	The "ouchless" bandage.

Crest toothpaste	Look ma, no cavities!
Colgate toothpaste	Clean your breath while you clean your teeth.
Crown books	If you paid full price, you didn't buy it at Crown.
Clorets	Don't broadcast bad breath.
Chanel No. 5	Every woman alive wants Chanel No. 5.
Coca Cola	The pause that refreshes.
Coca Cola	Things go better with Coke
Diet Coke	Just for the taste of it.
Dial Soap	Aren't you glad you use Dial? Don't you wish everybody did?
Downey Fabric Softener	April fresh.
DuPont	Better things for better living through chemistry.
Duracell	The coppertop battery
English Leather Aftershave	All my men wear English Leather . . . or they wear nothing at all
Eastern Airlines	Number one to the sun.
Eastern Airlines	We earn our wings everyday.
Foster Grant Sunglasses	Isn't that [celebrity] behind those Foster Grants?
Forbes Magazine	Capitalist tool.
Firestone tires	The name that's known is Firestone.
Ford	Ford has a better idea.
Folger's Coffee	It's mountain grown.
Gerber Baby Food	Babies are our business, our only business.
General Electric	Progress is our most important product.
General Electric	We bring good things to life.
Green Giant Foods	In the valley of the Jolly (ho-ho-ho) Green Giant.

Greyhound Bus	Go Greyhound—and leave the driving to us.
Gillette razors & blades	Look sharp! Feel sharp! Be sharp!
Holiday Inn	The nation's innkeeper
Hallmark Cards	When you care enough to send the very best.
Hertz Rent-a-Car	Let Hertz put you in the driver's seat.
E.F. Hutton	When E. F. Hutton talks, people listen.
IBM	Machines should work. People should think.
Ivory Soap	99 44/100 per cent pure.
Ivory Soap	It floats.
Jif Peanut Butter	Choosy mothers choose Jif.
Johnson's Baby Shampoo	No more tears.
Kellogg's Rice Krispies	Snap, crackle and pop.
Kentucky Fried Chicken	Finger lickin' good.
Kodak	Open me first.
Kodak	For the times of your life.
Levi's Action Slacks	Comfort fit for a man.
Levitz Furniture	You'll love it at Levitz.
Lipton Tea	The "brisk" tea
L'eggs Panty Hose	Nothing beats a great pair of L'eggs.
Lucky Strike Cigarettes	So round, so firm, so fully packed.
Lucky Strike Cigarettes	L.S.M.F.T. (Lucky Strike Means Fine Tobacco).
Marlboro Cigarettes	You get a lot to like with a Marlboro.
Marlboro Cigarettes	Come to Marlboro country.
Maxwell House Coffee	Good to the last drop.
Midway Airlines	Our spirit will lift you.
Memorex tape	Is it live or is it Memorex?
Mastercard	Master the possibilities.
McDonald's	You deserve a break today.
Merrill Lynch	Merrill Lynch is bullish on America.
Metropolitan Life	Get Met. It pays.
Miller Beer	If you've got the time, we've got the beer.

Miller High Life	The champagne of bottled beer.
M&M Candies	The chocolate melts in your mouth, not in your hand.
Morton Salt	When it rains, it pours.
Motel 6	We'll leave the light on for you.
Noxema Shave Cream	Take it off. Take it *all* off.
Noxema Cleansing Cream	Are you washing your face or drying your skin?
Nestea	Take the Nestea plunge.
Nestle's Chocolate	N-E-S-T-L-E-S, Nestle's makes the very best...chocolate.
Oldsmobile	It's a new generation of Olds.
Pepsi Cola	For those who think young.
Pepsi Cola	You're in the Pepsi generation.
Pepsi Cola	Take the Pepsi challenge.
Pall Mall Cigarettes	Outstanding . . . and they are mild.
Pepsodent Toothpaste	You'll wonder where the yellow went when you brush your teeth with Pepsodent.
Prince Spaghetti	Wednesday is Prince Spaghetti day.
Pepperidge Farm	Pepperidge Farm remembers.
Parker Pens	The world's most wanted pens.
Prudential Insurance	Get a piece of the rock.
Paul Masson Wines	We will sell no wine before its time.
Pabst Blue Ribbon Beer	What'll you have?
Playtex Bras	Cross your heart.
Pontiac	We build excitement.
Rolaids Antacid	How do you spell relief?
ReaLemon Lemon Juice	It's reconstituted.
Sharp Electronics	From Sharp minds come Sharp products.
Sealy Mattress	Like sleeping on a cloud.
Sara Lee	Nobody doesn't like Sara Lee.
Schlitz Beer	The beer that made Milwaukee famous.
Schlitz Beer	Go for the gusto.

State Farm Insurance	Like a good neighbor, State Farm is there.
Smith Barney	We make money the old fashioned way. We earn it.
7-UP	The Uncola.
7-UP	You like it. It likes you.
7-UP	Fresh up with 7-UP.
Tareyton Cigarettes	I'd rather fight than switch.
Toni Home Permanent	Which twin has the Toni?
Tums Antacid	Tums for the tummy.
Texaco	You can trust your car to the man who wears the star.
U.S. Army	Be all that you can be.
U.S. Marines	The Marines are looking for a few good men.
United Airlines	Fly the friendly skies.
United Negro College Fund	A mind is a terrible thing to waste.
U-Haul	Adventure in moving.
V-8 Vegetable Juice	I should've had a V-8.
Virginia Slims Cigarettes	You've come a long way, baby.
Wendy's	Where's the beef?
Wrigley's Double Mint Gum	Double your pleasure, Double your fun.
Westinghouse	You can be sure if it's Westinghouse.
Wheaties	Breakfast of Champions
Winston Cigarettes	Winston tastes good like a cigarette should.
Wonder Bread	Helps build strong bodies 12 ways.
Wisk Detergent	Ring around the collar.
Zenith	The quality goes in before the name goes on.

And here are a few not so classic lines that make you wonder what the creative people were thinking. How many can you remember?

The $6 List

Company	Slogan
McDonnell Douglas	We bring technology to life
FMC Pesticides	See no weevil . . . hear no weevil.
Honda Station Wagon	Even when it's empty it's loaded.
Dentyne	The gum that bites you back.
Pan Am	We fly the world the way the world wants to fly.
Antique Bourbon	The waterproof bourbon.
Chivas Regal	Give dad an expensive belt.
Northwest Airlines	Serving America's billionaires.
Sharp Electronics	If it isn't Sharp, it's dull.
Eve Cigarettes	Every inch a lady.
Trident Gum	Millions of teeth can't be wrong.
Maximum Car Speakers	Our woofers bark, but don't bite.
Pulsar	Why give an ordinary present when you can give someone goose bumps?
Old Gold Cigarettes	If you want a treat instead of a treatment, smoke Old Gold.
Marlboro Cigarettes	Ivory tips protect your lips.
Lender's Bagels	Bagel shop taste without the schlep.
IBM	Think.
Listerine	Often a bridesmaid, never a bride.
Old Gold Cigarettes	Not a cough in a carload.
Black Flag	Birth control for roaches.
Kraft Parmesan Cheese	Give your pasta a fair shake shaker.
Coca Cola	It had to be good to be where it is.
Triscuit Snack Crackers	Listen to your mouth.
Merrill Lynch	Ignoring this coupon could stunt your growth.
Levi's Jeans	134 years old and still on the bottom.
Jolt Cola	All the sugar and twice the caffiene.
Heinz Home Style Gravy	Close . . . but no lumps.

The Chicago Board of Trade asked investors to "Explore a Frontier as Fertile as our Heartland." (Courtesy of the Chicago Board of Trade. Used by permission.)

"Explore a frontier as vast as your imagination." (Courtesy of the Chicago Board of Trade. Used by permission.)

York Furrier found young love in this "Fall Classic." (Courtesy of York Furrier. Used by permission.)

York 🦊 Furrier

IMAGES *of* INDIVIDUALITY

Fall Classic.
"I suppose you're going to tell me basketball starts tomorrow."

Country Dyed Bassarisk Stroller.

Since the Thirties, York Furrier has stood for individual service.
Couldn't you stand a little?

York Furrier • Owned and operated by the Joseph R. Wagner family.
107 N. York Road • Elmhurst, IL • (312) 832-2200

All furs ranch-raised or government controlled and are labeled to show country of origin.

United Audio Centers found more than technical data in "The store for people who live for the music." (Courtesy of United Audio Centers. Used by permission.)

The store for people who live for the music.

Maybe it started years ago in your parents' den. Or a friend's bedroom. Or listening to a boombox at the beach.

One day you cranked up the music, and something inside you started to dance.

From then on you were hooked. You loved good music, and you would never stop looking for exhilarating ways to enjoy it.

For you, there are stores called United Audio Centers.

Our shelves resonate with the newest and the best—from Sony, Yamaha, Denon, Polk Audio,

Bang & Olufsen, Mitsubishi. And our floors boast a rare breed of salesperson. Who thoroughly understand the technology and help people make intelligent choices.

So come and listen with us. Listen as long as you like in our acoustically perfect rooms. Experience the thrill of large screen *"theater"* tv and surround sound. Come back again and again, if that's what it takes.

We'll help you take the next step up, maybe a big step up, in how you listen to your music.

And, after all, isn't *"the music"* what it's really all about?

Yamaha RX-530. The best-selling receiver from the world's largest manufacturer of quality musical instruments. **$399**

Denon DCM-555 II. Denon's 6-disc CD changer delivers many times the pleasure of conventional CD players without compromising a note. **$499**

Sony TCWR5ES. From Sony's acclaimed ES series comes a double cassette deck that's in tune with all the complexities of recording. **$429**

The right components for life.

UNITED**AUDIO**CENTERS

Audio Video Car Stereo

Brown's Chicken Restaurants found an unusual celebrity presenting this 30-second TV spot titled "Gorby Speaks!" (Courtesy Brown's Chicken Restaurants. Used by permission.)

Client: Brown's Chicken Restaurants
Product: Wednesday Special
Title: "Gorby Speaks"

Produced by: Weber Cohn & Riley
Comml. No.:   BC-8903-TV-15
Timing: 30 Seconds

1. (SFX: APPLAUSE)
GORBY: ...And let me take just a few moments to talk about Red's Chicken...Brown's Chicken.

2. Anyhow, here's the deal...

3. ten pieces of better tasting Brown's Chicken...

4. combined with a choice...

5. of many side dishes.

6. Oh boy!

7. When I see all this, bought by happy American families for just...

8. nine dollars and ninety-nine cents.

9. Well, from the very beginning, I thought this might be a device to entice consumer...

10. to enjoy Brown's Chicken at a very low price.

11. And now, I'm sure of it.

12. (SFX: APPLAUSE)
SINGER: BROWN'S CHICKEN IT TASTES BETTER.

The Fontana Spa promised "A Classic Restoration of Body and Spirit" in a series of print ads in major magazines and newspapers. (Courtesy the Abbey Group of Hotels. Used by permission.)

Van Kampen Merritt said the key to success was "Investing with a sense of direction." (Courtesy of Van Kampen Merritt. Used by permission.)

Direction.

These days, it's easy for investors to feel lost. Investment counselors are helping them find their way with mutual funds and unit trusts sponsored by Van Kampen Merritt—over $20 billion worth. Van Kampen Merritt is a Xerox Financial Services company offering a wide range of investment banking capabilities.

Before your clients invest or send money, have them obtain a prospectus which contains more complete information about charges and expenses. See the light. Call for more information about Van Kampen Merritt investment opportunities. **1-800-225-2222 ext. 6125, and visit our booth at the IAFD conference.**

Mutual Funds, Unit Trusts, Public and Health Care Finance, Capital Markets, Asset Management, Precious Metals, Xerox Life Products.

Van Kampen Merritt

A XEROX *Financial Services Company*

Investing with a sense of direction

Vision was a part of "Investing with a sense of direction."
(Courtesy of Van Kampen Merritt. Used by permission.)

Vision.

With the insight it takes to turn an investment opportunity into a
reality, Van Kampen Merritt sparks a wide variety of public and
private ventures to life. Our Capital Market Group provides
responsive, cost-efficient financing for projects, big and small. We
can bring to bear an impressive capital base and the considerable
resources of Xerox Financial Services. Yet, we remain accessible to
our clients throughout every phase of a transaction. It's made us
one of the fastest growing investment firms in the nation. Contact
us about your financing needs.

Van Kampen Merritt Capital Markets Group
Lisle, IL 1-800-225-2222 • Philadelphia, PA 1-800-523-4556

Van Kampen Merritt

A XEROX Financial Services Company

Investing with a sense of direction

Washington National Insurance Company advertised its restructuring and narrowing its business focus with "The Benefits of Being Narrow Minded." (Courtesy of Washington National Insurance Company. Used by permission.)

THE BENEFITS OF BEING NARROW- MINDED

Broad strokes can't paint a sharp picture. While some insurance companies try to be all things to all people, at Washington National we've decided there's a better approach. So we've narrowed our focus to provide broader benefits for you.

We've decided it would be healthier for us to concentrate on the health insurance needs of our customers—individually and in groups.

We're building on 78 years of leadership in these areas. And with 40 consecutive years of the highest possible ratings from A.M. Best, we have the strength and stability to deliver on our promises.

To get a broader view of Washington National's Individual Health, Group Health or Group Life products call 1/800/334-9038.

Some Hits . . . and Misses

A campaign for United Audio Centers focused on humor and attention-grabbing illustrations. That was okay, but when the ads included more detailed product information, albeit rather technical and esoteric, sales increased. That's what the buyer of a top-line sound system wanted—more information.

William Farley, CEO of Farley Industries, appeared in a television commercial, walking through a factory, speaking of how his company was working to meet the challenges of the future. For its production value it was a clean enough spot and Mr. Farley, a very articulate, nice-looking man . . . but so what? The spot failed to mention what Farley Industries did or sold (Fruit of the Loom underwear, among other things) and left viewers confused about why the spot was airing. Was Mr. Farley running for something? Was the company for sale? It might be reasonable to guess the commercial's aim was to enhance name awareness and interest in Farley stock. But a commercial that leaves viewers asking, "What was the point of that?," is a dubious achievement.

Confusion about advertising is not a new thing. Among the most commonly confused ads are those for political candidates where so much time is spent attacking a candidate's opponent that recall tests show the viewer was not certain which candidate had actually run the ad. Negative campaigns, as they are called, devote most of their time and space to listing the weaknesses of the competition, with the ad's sponsor coming in only at the end, as if coming over the hill, to the rescue, emerging from the clouds. The content of these ads is so poorly defined as to make them the subject of considerable criticism. One major reason this approach is used is because of the significant lack of *difference* between the candidates. If you can't find something unique and positive to say, the theory holds, devote your ad to the negatives of your competition. This style grew expansive in the 1980s, moving beyond political advertising.

Parity products have challenged ad agency creativity for years. As hard as some people might try, many still cannot find significant differences between Oldsmobile and Buick or Diet-Coke and Diet-Pepsi or Tide and Fab or Colgate and Ultra-Brite. The battle for market share and brand loyalty heats up: much of the public, when ready to choose, say they just can't seem to see enough difference between products to justify a certain price or help them choose for reasons other than cost.

Sex, Humor, Celebrities

The creative method of differentiating products often has involved elements of our culture that have historically been the great differentiators: sex, celebrities and humor.

First the Sex . . .

Which aftershave will you buy when they all seem pretty much the same? Why, the one that drove the beautiful woman crazy in the ad, of course. This is an example of carrying the "show the benefits of the product" rule to its furthest limits.

The common adage is that *sex sells*. It's hard to argue with that. Whether suggestive or blatant, ads with sexual content get attention and are remembered. Models have built fabulous careers and seven-figure incomes on the basis of nothing more than looking beautiful in an ad. Not brassy or flashy, just beautiful. They may represent objects of desire or role models, but the important thing to the advertiser is that you noticed . . . and now that we've got your attention, a word about our product.

American television has always maintained a level of censorship when it comes to obvious sex in advertising, more so than its print or European counterparts. Until the 1980s, women's undergarments virtually were shown while still in their packaging. Magazines had women dreaming of conquering the world in Maidenform bras and showed it happening. TV barely suggested it. Jim Palmer in his Jockey shorts made it to billboards and *People* magazine, but not the living room tube.

But for all of it prudishness and fear of pressure from the religious right, TV has not been against sexual subtlety—the woman luxuriating in her bath, the couple's smoldering glances over a bottle of wine. The question isn't as much, "Can you see yourself in this picture?" as it is, "Would you *like* to be in this picture?" If so, the product promises to be of great benefit to you.

An ad for a jeweler wanted to sell gems that looked exactly like diamonds, but were not. The photo in the ad showed a barechested woman with a surprised expression and the headline, "You mean these aren't real?" The ad conjures up an image of a jeweler and an ad agency team, cigar stubs in their mouths, elbowing each other's ribs and having a laugh. That is to say, a low-class feeling. The ad received considerable attention. How much jewelry the ad sold is something else.

Lear's magazine wanted to make a point: women don't stop being beautiful or sexy when they pass forty or fifty years of age. With taste and subtlety, the *Lear's* ad series showed mature women in elegant, non-provocative semi-nude poses, as strikingly attractive as the *Cosmopolitan* magazine girls half their age at the other end of the newsstand.

Calvin Klein has always had strong sexually provocative advertising. Does it work? Sales increased some 300 percent after the first ads appeared with Brooke Shields in her Calvin Klein jeans. Male and female nudes in Obsession perfume print ads and television spots that smoldered with sensuality were maddeningly confusing, controversial, and effective. They achieved the ultimate two tributes: people asked one another if they had seen them, and they sold a lot of perfume.

Like so much else in the creative process, the degree to which sex or sexuality might be used to good effect as a way to get attention and be remembered is very subjective.

Again, David Ogilvy: "The first advertisement I ever produced showed a naked woman. It was a mistake, not because it was sexy, but because it was irrelevant to the product—a cooking stove. The test is *relevance*."

The argument about sex in advertising won't be settled quickly, particularly if Wilson Bryan Key has anything to say about it. Professor Key has turned sex-in-advertising into a virtual cottage industry with speeches, seminars and at least three books on the subject. His conviction is that advertisers bury "subliminal" images, mainly sexual, within an ad or commercial. These images are received by the subconscious mind without the viewer of the ad realizing it. His books offer a collective example of some fifty pages of such ads. At the risk of appearing argumentative, we have never met anyone in the industry who has done this; we doubt the practice exists, and we feel that Professor Key's pages of enlarged "sex" photos are in fact innocuous.

In his book *Subliminal Seduction*, he writes "Within the multidimensional Cinzano ice cubes the designs can mean virtually anything the reader wishes to fantasize and project. Projections, however, quite often involve some form of sexual fantasy. In the Cinzano cubes the artist has included subtle cues which will lead the reader, at both the conscious and unconscious levels, to interpret male or female genital symbols, breasts, nude couples, animals—the possibilities are endless."

Indeed.

Some people have observed various faces, objects and other formations in clouds, trees, ink blots, and the occasional snowdrift—without the help of ad agencies trying to "subliminally" sell them anything. Still, the rumor persists that the "man in the moon" Proctor &

Gamble logo is a thinly disguised symbol of Satanic intention.

If your agency suggests using subliminal techniques in your ads (a pretty far-fetched, if not bizarre, likelihood), get another agency, one that employs attractive models in its ads rather than trying to spell "sex" in hair curls.

Creating desire for your products by creating desirable scenes into which the audience members may project themselves is a captivating advertising approach. Sex, tastefully, maturely included, may help get attention, but without a benefit to the customer, it still won't make a sale.

This Better Be Funny

Humor, on the other hand, is no laughing matter when it comes to your advertising. Every year when awards are handed out for the best ads, the funny ones usually walk away with the honors. To name ten:

> Federal Express: "Fast Talker"
> Wendy's: "Where's the Beef?"
> Diet Coke: "Roger Rabbit"
> Bud Light: "Spuds MacKenzie"
> Coca Cola: "Max Headroom"
> Bartles & Jaymes: "Wine Coolers"
> Eveready Energizer: "The Bunny"
> Nike: "Michael Jordan/Spike Lee"
> Volkswagen: "Uncle Max's Funeral"
> Jell-O: "Bill Cosby & Kids"

If creative work is subjective, humor is clearly the most subjective aspect of all. It is particularly challenging because not everyone thinks the same things are funny. As times change, humor, like music and hairstyles, change with them. The Jerry Lewis style of comedy gives way to Monty Python, to David Letterman, and on and on. When you elect to use humor, you likely eliminate major segments of your target group.

Alliance Financial Corporation ran an ad showing a platoon of men in gray business suits seated around a conference table, all wearing the false-nose-with-glasses-and-mustache sold in novelty stores. The idea was to show the audience Alliance wasn't pompous and they didn't take themselves too seriously. Well, their audience *wanted* them to take themselves seriously. As one viewer commented, "Who wants to trust their money to guys who come on like a bunch of clowns?" Somebody's idea of a funny ad wasn't funny to someone else.

Why do so many advertisers use humor, then?

Because, again, in a field of parity products, it is particularly effective at distinguishing *your* product. Some people may not think the Energizer bunny is funny, but they may still remember the name—associating it with an image. Second, even if the public doesn't think an ad is funny, there is a mentality that looks favorably on those who don't take themselves too seriously. Amid the hollow, pompous, generic claims of quality, value, service, new, improved, and we're number one, a humorous ad is a breath of fresh air. Third, unless the ad is absolutely terrible, just doing it at all is good for awareness and awareness translates to market share.

Remember always that humor about drunks isn't funny anymore. Alcoholism is too great a modern social concern. "Guy goes into a bar . . ." stories don't make it in advertising. The same holds true for humor at the expense of religion or ethnicity. No matter how inoffensive the joke or its intention, there are pressure groups ready to call a press conference and hit the picket lines at the first appearance of a priest, a nun, a rabbi, Italian peddler, Irish cop, or Iranian cab driver. Humorous advertising has gone from creatively challenging to risky business.

But, if the ad is perceived as being *good*, a humorous ad is *better* than a straight ad. People remember funny lines, repeat them and tell others about the comical new commercial.

Star Power

Besides sex and comedy, *stars sell*. They may be from movies, television, politics, music, theatre or sports, but a familiar face and voice will get attention, be remembered, and help identify your brand with some presence other than just one more of the same in the category.

Usually.

The greatest concern in using a celebrity presenter was always that the star might upstage the product by being better known than what they are selling. Cher's perfume is called *Uninhibited*, yet consumers remember it as *Cher's perfume*.

But a new celebrity presenter dilemma came out of the 1980s. Some called it *Star Wars*.

Pepsi signs Michael Jackson.

So Coke signs George Michael, the Pointer Sisters, and a few others.

Pepsi signs Madonna . . . and so on.

The result is that the borrowed interest, the presence the celebrity was to bring, has been watered down by the presence of too many celebrities hawking too many products. The identification with the star becomes thin. The audience has trouble recalling who's pitching what. Furthermore, celebrities already accustomed to changing record companies, studios, and networks put little premium on loyalty. Several have been known to "jump brands," negating their value to a great degree.

Recent research also indicates that, while the public enjoys seeing stars, they know the star's services are for sale and don't take their endorsements all that seriously.

You're sitting with your agency people, feeling pretty smug at having just received something between a fine and a great campaign when the question arises: who will appear in the ad—an "anybody" or a "star"? This decision can have enormous—expensive—consequences.

Advertising has always been a fascinating two-way path for the famous. Many of our most celebrated performers got their first major public exposure in TV commercials or print ads (such as an unknown Dustin Hoffman as a pitchman for Volkswagen). Others "ended up" in ads as their careers abated (such as television and film actress Dorothy Provine).

At another level is the top-dollar/top-name celebrity whose costly presence in an ad is expected to garner greater attention and greater sales. Sometimes it is the talent the celebrity brings that influences the ad; other times it is "borrowed interest." An audience segment is not necessarily interested in a diet or weight loss program, but *is* interested in actress Jane Fonda. The audience thus will watch a television commercial (or read an ad) in which Ms. Fonda is featured presenting videos, records, or club memberships for weight loss programs. That's an example of borrowed interest. Other of the most common uses of borrowed interest are using baseball to sell beer or using scenes from old movies to promote a fast-food restaurant.

Former First Lady Nancy Reagan appeared in public service announcements. Regardless of your politics, the wife of the President of the United States coming on the air with an announcement took on an aura of importance and got your attention. When a spokesperson's position is so cloaked in dignity, *any* appearance is considered significant.

For years some actors or public officials would not appear in ads because it carried the suggestion that a) they needed the money or exposure; b) they were behaving in an undignified manner; or c) both of the above.

Public service ads were the exception. Such spots as Marlon Brando for United States Savings Bonds, Paul Newman recruiting foster parents, or Elizabeth Taylor soliciting for a worthy charity were often done for no fee and were considered good career moves.

Mostly, however, celebrities were and are used in advertising on the promise that their presence will deliver a larger audience for the ad than that of an unknown actor or model. And that's worth a large fee to the advertiser. Right?

       *   *   *   *   *

Sometimes. At the risk of stating the obvious, a star alone won't make a bad ad good.

Cher, Victoria Principal, and Heather Locklear generate much more interest in health and fitness clubs than the ads featuring "Charlie," the founder of the Charlie Club.

The Rolling Stones, Frank Sinatra, and Phil Collins TV commercials for various beers keep more people from leaving the room or switching channels than the spots featuring unknown models standing at the bar.

George C. Scott for Renault was a flop.

John Wayne for Datril pain reliever gave people a headache.

Cybill Sheperd and James Garner (in separate spots) proved embarrassing to the Beef Council. (She's a vegetarian. He underwent bypass surgery for blocked arteries, a condition frequently equated to high levels of fat in one's diet.)

Bill Cosby, one of America's most effective and successful commercial spokesmen proved highly *in*effective for E. F. Hutton.

Pop stars Michael Jackson and Madonna and vice presidential candidate Geraldine Ferraro caused many Pepsi stockholders to wonder what the company's management could have been up to with ads that generated millions of dollars of publicity . . . and controversy.

Chrysler CEO Lee Iacocca became nationally recognized doing his own "straight-talk" ads.

Victor Kaim of Remington did not.

CEO William Farley for Farley Industries (Fruit of the Loom) became a curiosity.

*   *   *   *   *

The value of the celebrity presenter has long been the subject of debate in advertising.
Consider:

- What percent of your ad budget or production cost goes to the celebrity?

- Is your spokesperson better known than your product?

- Can you count on your celebrity reflecting positively on your company or product in future career decisions?

This does not attempt to present a lopsided argument *against* the celebrity, but it does urge careful evaluation of a potentially costly move.

Few in advertising would argue that Bill Cosby and *Jell-O* was a great, if not, inspired pairing. John Houseman recreating the persona of his Academy Award-winning Professor Kingsfield of "The Paper Chase" intoning that brokerage firm Smith Barney "Makes money the old-fashioned way—we *earn* it," made the old conservative firm virtually a pop institution for the 1980s.

And countless advertisers over the years learned that such broadcast luminaries as Arthur Godfrey and Dick Clark were worth the extra money paid them to put their products on the map.

But good, ultimately effective advertising begins with a plan . . . and with questions like, "What is it we want to accomplish here?"

Maximum exposure for the product name? If we don't spend half the budget on a star can we afford more media placements, or is less more? That is to say, is one billboard with Cosby's face and our product name more effective than ten magazine ads with an unknown (or no) model?

The answer is a resounding "Maybe."

What are the ten magazines?

What's the art in the ad?

Is the copy crisp, easy to read, entertaining or useful information?

Does the ad create an impact that stops the audience, grabs attention and is long remembered?

Sometimes, of course, it all comes down to a function of budget: you can't afford a recognizable celebrity. Then there are the exceptions:

*   *   *   *   *

Blackglama Furs used some of Hollywood's most glamorous stars for its successful "What becomes a legend most . . .?" print campaign. The story goes that, while the company's budget didn't allow for the stars' large fees, if they would agree to pose wearing the coat, they could keep those coats in lieu of the fee. The campaign was successful in that it identified Blackglama with the preeminent names in other fields. Not just glamorous, but *important*. An elegant fur coat has always suggested status; *this* brand of fur suggested status among those having the highest status.

*   *   *   *   *

Frank Sinatra is said to have been so impressed with Chrysler Chairman Lee Iacocca's tireless efforts to save the failing auto company that he offered to appear in a series of straight-talk ads and TV commercials with Iacocca, appealing to America's patriotism to choose Chrysler over foreign competitors. His fee for the appearances was a reported one dollar. The campaign succeeded not so much in making the Chrysler case as a better choice of car, but in that good Americans should rally to the cause and help save this company that represented tens of thousands of jobs and America's prestige around the world as well. It worked as a part of one of the great business turnarounds in American history.

Perhaps the reigning champion of curious celebrity advertising choices is singer Michael Jackson. Only a year after entering into a $10 million/three-year deal with Pepsi—a matter that became the top story on the evening news for weeks—the singer entered into a reported $20 million deal with clothing and footwear manufacturer L.A. Gear. (No fee is revealed or estimated for Mr. Jackson's allowing a "claymation" figure of himself, a kind of animated puppet, to be used in the TV commercials of the "California Raisins").

Mr. Jackson's Pepsi ads were particularly interesting as a study in the use of celebrities in advertising for a number of reasons, not the least of which involve the enormous money paid the star. Certainly one doesn't engage a performer of this magnitude and cut corners on production values. Estimates ran as high as $1 million for each of the first three TV spots produced under the contract.

More interesting than the astronomical contract was the fact that Michael Jackson was widely known to *not* be a consumer of cola beverages. Further, his arrangement with the advertiser allowed that he not be required to either say the product name or appear in the same picture with the product. So here was a major star being paid an enormous sum to appear in a commercial for a product—but not *with* the product—that the audience knows he doesn't use or even mention!

And, by virtually all accounts, the deal was considered a success. It seems Mr. Jackson's fans worldwide were delighted to get a look at him and were grateful to Pepsi for making it happen. No matter that he didn't use their product; they apparently had no problem with that. Their logic was, essentially, Pepsi is Michael Jackson's cola whether he drinks it or not. It would be virtually impossible to put a dollar amount on the publicity that surrounded the deal. *USA Today* and *People* magazine, two media avenues numbering more than a few cola drinkers among their readers, wrote, rewrote and followed the event *ad nauseam.* What did Michael's fans think? How would Coke respond? Who would be the next celebrity ad star?

Curiously, the next major ad superstar signed to a multi-million dollar deal was pop singer Madonna . . . for Pepsi. In a format similar in concept to that used for Michael Jackson, a rock video spot, Madonna was featured in a commercial similar to the video for her latest record. The record was the subject of considerable controversy from various conservative organizations, who described it as being everything from irreverent to blasphemous. Similarly, the commercial came under attack. Protests were lodged and boycotts of Pepsi threatened. The company pulled the spot, saying it was not bowing to pressure, but was reconsidering its use of the commercial and Madonna. Meanwhile, again, enormous publicity was generated in newspapers, on radio and on television— both on news shows and talk shows such as *Today* and *Good Morning America.*

The enormous amount of attention for Pepsi is, of course, great in terms of enhancing brand awareness and recognition. The big question, of course, is did it sell Pepsi Cola? The company seems to believe that over the long haul they will benefit from all of the attention and the identification with personalities such as Michael Jackson and Madonna—in many respects, symbols of the consumer group they seek to attract.

The jury is not in on this type of approach to advertising overall. Few advertisers have ad budgets the size of Pepsi's, budgets that allow for paying more to a single celebrity than most advertisers spend for media over several years. And no one, of course, would dispute the fact that a company can spend its money however it pleases.

The overall strategy of identifying the product with the present and emerging generation of consumers is solid. Is it, however, a good long-term strategy to be an advertiser that simply spends money on talent, perhaps drawing the focus of attention away from the product, the *reason* for the ad to exist? The Michael Jackson Pepsi spot has clearly come a long way from singer Perry Como, thirty years earlier, taking a long puff on his Chesterfield cigarette and telling his audience, "That's my brand."

Every course on advertising, of course, admonishes students to never lose sight of the goal: *sell the product*. The use of the celebrity presenter in advertising has historically been the quickest way to achieve high visibility and recall. It has also been among the most expensive routes to use and runs the highest risk of having the product overshadowed in its own ad.

"Of course I remember the former Speaker of the House of Representatives in that commercial where he pops out of a suitcase," you may say; "I just can't seem to remember if it was for Samsonite or Holiday Inn."

It was for *Quality Inns*.

And the same retired government official, "Tip" O'Neill, appeared the same year in other ads for American Express, Miller Lite, Commodore Business Machines, The Trump Shuttle and the Bank of New England. Is Mr. O'Neill a believable spokesman for these advertisers? Is his presence likely to attract more consumers to the advertisers' message than high-tech graphics or a studio announcer? Most importantly, does the advertiser benefit from his appearance relative to his fee?

There are those who will argue that Visa could have bought a lot of four-color spreads in *Time* and *Newsweek* to make its case for the reported $8.5 million it paid singer Paul McCartney to appear in its ads. Does the company really believe Mr. McCartney's fans holding American Express cards, Discover cards, or MasterCards will only charge his albums and their designer jeans with

Visa because of his presence in their ads? Was landing him a coup worthy of note?

Sure.

Eight and a half million dollars worthy of note?

Unlikely.

Bill Cosby has had a more powerful impact on consumers with his Jell-O commercials than any ad campaign the company has run since its historic (though long forgotten) jingle in spots where the product name was spelled out to music.

Catherine Deneuve has made a lot of people remember Chanel perfume.

Farrah Fawcett not only sold a lot of shampoo and conditioner, but she left American women copying her hair style as well.

Joe DiMaggio, the baseball legend, had at least one generation of kids thinking his name was Mr. Coffee.

In each of these cases the company ad director can take a bow and, clearly, the agency guessed right.

But can we really believe the presence of Priscilla and Lisa Marie Presley in an Oldsmobile spot sent people racing to the nearest Olds showroom?

Or that we filled up with Amoco because the Lone Ranger did?

Ray Charles for Kentucky Fried Chicken?

If you use a celebrity in your ad; your guiding rules should be:

1   Does the celebrity complement or overshadow your product?

2   Will this celebrity be someone you want consumers to identify with your product now and continue associating with your product long after the campaign is history?

3   Do you have contractual assurances that the celebrity will not appear in an ad for a competitor within a reasonable period? (A big problem in the "cola wars" campaigning during which Coke's and Pepsi's celebrities have been known to move from one product to another.)

4   Is the celebrity overexposed in ads and commercials (do the names Ed McMahon, Dick Clark and Mike Ditka come to mind)?

5   Is this celebrity's fee worth more to you than the cost of a competent "unknown" actor or model?

Remember, Arthur Godfrey virtually single-handedly made Lipton's the tea of choice in America for two generations. And James Garner, who also promoted beef, joined with Marriette Hartley to make the country believe Polaroid cameras were great fun to own and use.

But what was that car George C. Scott tried to sell me again? All of the celebrities listed below appeared in print and/or broadcast ads. Some of them found greater success and recognition from selling than from the exposure which originally gained them celebrity status. Many truly contributed to the memorable quality of the ads. Others should have caused the ad agencies involved to rethink how they spend their clients' money. Of the following 100 or so celebrities in ads, how many do you remember? Were they assets or liabilities to the ads? Or were they without any effect whatsoever?

The critical question, of course, is *were they worth* it (almost any amount)? Did they help the products?

Celebrity	*Advertiser*
Paula Abdul	Diet Coke
Edie Adams	Muriel Cigars
Mason Adams	Smuckers
Alan Alda	Atari, IBM
Herb Alpert	Listen Perfume
Paul Anka	Kodak
Frankie Avalon	Oldsmobile
Lucille Ball and Desi Arnaz	Phillip Morris
Harry Belefonte	Oldsmobile
Candace Bergen	American Express, Sprint
Pat Boone	Chevrolet, milk

George Burns	[numerous]
Dick Cavett	[numerous]
Cher	health clubs, perfume
Ray Charles	Kentucky Fried Chicken, American Express
Dick Clark	[numerous]
Phil Collins	Michelob
William Conrad	First Alert
Bill Cosby	Jell-O, Coke, Ford, Kodak, E.F. Hutton; others
Betty Davis	Lux
Rodney Dangerfield	Miller Light
Catherine Deneuve	Chanel Perfume
Joe DiMaggio	Mr. Coffee
Bob Denver	McDonald's
Mike Ditka	Midway Airlines; others
Sheena Easton	health clubs
Linda Evans	Crystal Light; others
Farrah Fawcett	[numerous]
Geraldine Ferraro	Diet Pepsi
Annette Funicello	Skippy Peanut Butter, Kentucky Fried Chicken
Michael J. Fox	Diet Pepsi
James Garner	Polaroid, Mazda, Beef
Peter Graves	Oldsmobile; others
Lorne Greene	Alpo; others
Meriette Hartley	Polaroid, Celestial Seasons Teas
Helen Hayes	American Express
Hal Holbrook	Sears Financial Network
Bob Hope	Buick
John Houseman	Smith Barney; others
Dustin Hoffman	Volkswagen
Sen. Sam Irvin	American Express
David Jannsen	Excedrin
Elton John	Diet Coke
Don Johnson	Diet Coke
The Judds	Oldsmobile

Michael Jordan	Nike; others
Michael Jackson	Pepsi, California Raisins, L.A. Gear
Jack Klugman	Eagle Snacks, Canon Copiers
Dr. Arthur Laffer, Economist	Cadillac
Burt Lancaster	MCI
Spike Lee	Nike
Jack Lemmon	Union
Jay Leno	Doritos
Heather Locklear	health clubs
Sophia Loren	Lux
Jackie Mason	Honda
Madonna	Pepsi
Mickey Mantle	Brut
Paul McCartney	Visa
Ed McMahon	[numerous]
Demi Moore	Diet Coke
Jim McMahon	Honda; others
George Michael	Coke
Joe Namath	[numerous]
Hon. Tip O'Neill	Trump Airlines, American Express; others
Paul Newman	American Express
Donny & Marie Osmond	Hawaiian Punch
Jim Palmer	Jockey Underwear
Merlin Olssen	FTD Florists
Priscilla Presley	Oldsmobile; others
The Pointer Sisters	Coke
Victoria Principal	Jhirmack, health clubs
Ronald Reagan	GE, US Borax, Chesterfield Cigarettes
Lynn Redgrave	Weight Watchers
Donna Rice	Guess Jeans
Christopher Reeve	MCI, Guess Jeans
Lionel Ritchie	Pepsi
Tony Randall	[numerous]
Cliff Robertson	AT&T

The Rolling Stones	Budweiser
George C. Scott	Renault
Dinah Shore	Chevrolet; others
William Shatner	Oldsmobile, Promise Margarine
Cybill Shepherd	L'Oreal, Beef
O.J. Simpson	Hertz
Frank Sinatra	Chrysler, Revlon, Michelob
Smothers Brothers	Magnavox, Stouffer's
Jaclyn Smith	K-Mart; others
Suzzane Sommers	Ace Hardware
Ringo Starr	Wine Coolers, Oldsmobile
Connie Stevens	Ace Hardware
Meryl Streep	American Express
Elizabeth Taylor	Passion Perfume
Roy Thinnes	[numerous]
Donald Trump	Pepsi, Trump Game
Tina Turner	Chrysler
Mike Tyson	Pepsi; others
John Wayne	Datril
Bruce Willis	Seagram's
Steve Winwood	Michelob
Stevie Wonder	AT&T

American celebrities in foreign ads.

Paul Newman	Fuji Card [a Japanese Charge Card]
Madonna	Mitsubishi Hi-Fi Video
Rob Lowe	Suzuki Cultus Auto
George Lucas	Panasonic Technics
Gene Hackman	Kirin Beer
Mickey Rourke	Daihatsu Charade Auto
Thelonius Monk	Human Spice [Japanese Tobacco]

*   *   *   *   *

Some Ad Campaigns That Worked

The Chicago Board of Trade is the oldest and largest commodity futures exchange in the world.

The scene there is often intimidating, usually portrayed in newsphotos and on television as the center of aggressive behavior: crowds of men with arms outstretched, thrusting, waving, their faces contorted, shouting—screaming—and frantically communicating with mysterious, esoteric hand signals. The subject matter of the scene is itself no less foreign: futures contracts. Unlike the already somewhat complex business of trading stocks and bonds, which at least offers unsophisticated observers a simplistic overview (you buy or sell an interest in a company at one price, then you may alter your position at a later date, thereby taking a profit or incurring a loss), "futures" contracts have a totally different language. They are typical buy-and-sell type investment products (such as soy beans and pork bellies, foreign currencies, and precious metals).

The Chicago Board of Trade had a need to promote itself—but also a reluctance to do so.

More than 130 years old and historically the dominant force in its industry around the world, the exchange was experiencing (sometimes even being overshadowed by) competition from its hometown rival, the Chicago Mercantile Exchange. While the Board of Trade had led the way in futures trading, the Mercantile Exchange's introduction of the International Monetary Market had broadened futures trading interest from the farm to the much larger worldwide financial products playing field. Other exchanges in New York and Kansas City were becoming increasingly aggressive. Further, the market in futures trading was becoming a subject of great concern among legislators and regulators. Unlike the securities industry, governed by the strict oversight of the Securities and Exchange Commission, the nuances of the workings of the futures market were known only to industry professionals and a handful of knowledgeable persons in government. This situation prompted public remarks by government officials and journalists calling for tighter controls to insure protection for public investors.

Traditionally, the Chicago Board of Trade had run advertising programs that either announced the introduction of new products and trading facilities or offered seminar schedules. Few ads were really directed at *selling* the public on futures, and fewer still at enhancing the exchange's image. In fact there was at some level at the exchange a real *aversion* to image advertising. Many members felt the exchange that virtually invented the market should not have to advertise. Their attitude was that if the investing public didn't understand futures to a sufficient extent to benefit from the opportunities afforded, they might be better off out of the market altogether. However, this position was not interpreted as one aimed at protecting investors; rather, it was considered elitist, intended to keep the market an exclusive club.

The Chicago Board of Trade needed to enhance and improve its standing among regulators, legislators, investment firms, and the general public.

A major public relations effort was launched with literature, tapes, seminars, and speakers sent out around the country.

An advertising campaign was created to provide specific product information to all segments of the audience (investors, brokers, and the government), presented in a way intended to change people's minds about the exchange.

The first ad in the series showed a warm, restful landscape of a farm—green grass, trees, golden fields of corn and wheat—and carried the headline, *Explore a Frontier as Fertile as Our Heartland . . . the Chicago Board of Trade*. The copy in the ad was very specific on the benefits of futures contracts on agricultural commodities. The ads appeared in *The Wall Street Journal* and (usually in four-color) in major business publications including *Busi-*

ness Week, Fortune, and *Forbes* as well as selected industry trade publications such as *Futures, Agrifinance,* and trade association publications. A *Media Network* magazine buy carried the ad to a selected number of cities in certain targeted editions of *Time, Newsweek, U.S. News, Money,* and *Sports Illustrated.* The cumulative effect was that the ad seemed to be everywhere, while it appeared actually only in certain cities, certain editions, and a finely tuned list of high-visibility publications carefully targeted to the desired audiences. Additionally, 8 x 12-foot backlit reproductions of the ad offered a welcoming presence throughout Chicago's O'Hare International Airport.

A second ad showed a dramatic photograph of the earth in space against a dark starry sky. The headline was *Explore a Frontier as Vast as Your Imagination,* and the copy was specific about the benefits of futures contracts on (non-agricultural) financial instruments.

A third ad, for the Major Market Stock Index contract, used a bold, colorful photo of a rolling ocean with the headline *Explore a Frontier as Vast as the Ocean . . . without a Vast Fortune.* Like the farm scene, the financial instruments ads ran in major business and general news media with specific appropriate trade magazines supplementing the schedule.

The three ads used stock photography that proved to be extremely cost-effective and, because of its richness and artful look, set a tone and feeling not previously identified with the Board of Trade.

Further, using animation techniques, the stock color photographs were later filmed and, accompanied by excellent narration in the familiar voice of broadcaster and recording artist Ken Nordine (with a synthesizer background), the campaign moved to television. A well-negotiated purchase of time on cable's *Financial News Network,* with supplemental buys on *Cable News Network* and, in spot markets, on *Face the Nation* and *This Week with David Brinkley,* gave the impression that the exchange was spending a fortune, increasing its visibility in all major media. In fact, all media was negotiated well; although it "looked" like the exchange had spent millions the final bills actually came to a fraction of the imagined amount.

The *objective* of the "Explore a Frontier . . ." campaign was to cause nervous or negative brokers, investors, and government officials to say," I don't think I've ever actually thought of the Board of Trade in those terms," and stress the point that the futures market afforded tremendous opportunities for profit and for risk management.

The *resulting* campaign ran more than four years and included a dozen different print ads and three television commercials, a direct mail component and airport terminal adaptations. It markedly increased visibility and awareness and won numerous awards. Other exchanges raced to produce their own "image" ads, using television and airport visuals for the first time in *their* history. While it is often difficult to quantify this type of success, no one disputes the value of a number of brokerage firms, traditionally at arm's length from the exchange, displaying poster reproductions of the ads in their offices. The highly successful program was accomplished with an ad budget about half the size of that of its leading competitor.

In terms of its working relationship with its agency, some egos had to be put on "hold" for the campaign to succeed. The Chicago Board of Trade operates under a committee system. Each product (muni bonds, precious metals, agricultural options, financial instruments) had its own committee, and each committee had an exchange staff person responsible for product marketing. That staff person was charged with carrying out the product committee's directives and reported to an exchange senior vice president who, in turn, received all product committee concerns and directives and interacted with a more encompassing exchange marketing committee, which needed to coordinate all efforts while remaining consistent with the objectives and tone set by the executive committee and the Board of Directors, who were to reflect the will of the exchange's several thousand members—both individuals and trading firms.

It seemed like a wholly unworkable situation. The first questions one might consider are, how could an agency operate within such a maze . . . and why would one want to try?

The answer to the second question is because, to quote Hyman Roth to Michael Corleone in *The Godfather*, "This is the life we've chosen." (The more mercenary among us might note that one's compensation rises in direct relation to one's blood pressure.)

The first question was addressed by the client recognizing that, given the multitude of managers, committees, subcommittees, the board, and members involved—each of whom expected their opinions to be heard—there would have to be a workable system that would allow reviews and approvals to take place in this lifetime. The agency, for its part, had to recognize that its first task was to *listen*: so many people with so much to say meant *a lot* of listening.

The agency's account supervisor, account executive, executive creative director and art director attended meetings of each product committee, listening and taking notes. In creative strategy meetings back at the agency the "Explore a Frontier . . ." theme line was created as a statement about opportunities that lie ahead in the unknown and as an umbrella for the campaign. The line and visuals would establish the continuity of the campaign and the copy in each ad would reflect points the committees deemed important to present.

The exchange's vice president in charge of advertising was invited to many of the agency's strategy meetings. He was first to review the copy and rough layouts, offering suggestions and comments regarding points that might be politically noteworthy (what phrase might turn off certain members or what might be an extremely pleasing or displeasing point to the regulators). Comps were then presented by the agency to the senior vice president of marketing (the senior staff person) and the ad subcommittee. The exchange's vice president of advertising was present and acknowledged that he was involved in the campaign and endorsed it. Upon consensus approval of this group the work was produced in final form and shown by the marketing VP to members of the various committees and exchange staff, who had all agreed to abide by the decision of the advertising subcommittee. Since they probably have as many opinions as they have people, they recognized *somebody* had to make a decision. That somebody was designated and so empowered.

The ads ran and they worked.

*   *   *   *   *

Brown's Chicken Restaurants is the number two fast food chicken franchise in the greater Chicago area (after Kentucky Fried Chicken). With a tongue-in-cheek nod to *perestroika* and the whole idea of celebrity endorsers, Brown's capitalized on Soviet Party leader Gorbachev's visit to the United States—an event covered by the media virtually around the clock—by "borrowing" news conference footage of Mr. Gorbachev, and featuring a soundtrack in which he is barely able to contain his excitement over his discovery of Brown's ten-piece, $9.99 value dinner. The thirty-second spot sold quality and value with good humor and it also sold chicken...and spawned an array of imitators.

*   *   *   *   *

Actor David Leisure was introduced as "Joe Isuzu," making performance claims for Isuzu automobiles that were literally unbelievable—particularly when the screen carried the caption "He's lying," and other true information about the vehicle's performance. This send-up of inflated claims by unctuous auto dealers was the refreshing, entertaining, memorable talk of the auto industry in 1986.

The public responded by believing Isuzu had to be a quality product to risk poking fun at itself in this way and sales gains followed.

*   *   *   *   *

Director Joe Sedelmaier became briefly as famous as his client, *Wendy's*, with his thirty-second TV commercial featuring a group of elderly women comparing small burgers and large burger buns. The spot was actually titled "Fluffy Buns." But it was Clara Peller's wondering aloud, "Where's the beef?," in a gravelly, eighty-year old voice that was credited with launching a new national catchphrase and, incidentally, helping Wendy's sales increase some 32 percent.

*   *   *   *   *

People will be talking about Apple Computer's 1984 TV commercial (called "1984") for many years to come. When the three other campaigns (Brown's Chicken, Isuzu, Wendy's) won smiles and sales, they broke the rules to a degree by not taking themselves too seriously in a sea of advertising noted largely for doing just the opposite. Apple, however—in introducing its Macintosh PC in a stark, cold, futuristic sixty-second spot—made no attempt to make the audience feel good. It jarred audiences . . . and it certainly got their attention.

What all of these spots have in common is a client's willingness to take some chances, to trust the agency to risk offending some people, but produce powerful, effective advertising.

*   *   *   *   *

Van Kampen Merritt, the subject of the focus group interview noted earlier, is an emerging investment firm. Believing they needed to be more aggressive, the firm retained a new ad agency in 1987. The agency set out in two directions: first, conducting research to determine the level of awareness and recognition of the firm, both within its own industry and among members of the investing public; second, reviewing all available ads and collaterals the company had produced, looking for something upon which to build. Research revealed extremely low public awareness of the firm. Since the agency subscribed to the theory that there is a direct correlation between the level of awareness and the share of market, the first goal was to achieve a higher level of public awareness. A common perception, too, is that a company or product that is *better known* is a *better* company or product. By becoming better known, Van Kampen Merritt would indirectly raise perceptions of its quality level.

A review of previously produced materials found an illustration of a lighthouse on some pieces of literature. On other pieces, the firm declared its objective was "investing with a sense of direction."

The agency could have started from scratch, but in these two discoveries they identified the seeds of both an ad campaign and a motto/slogan/theme for the firm. "Investing with a Sense of Direction," symbolized by a lighthouse, would become the Van Kampen Merritt message.

The creative approach was an example of the expression "less is more," in that the single word "Direction" above a color photo of a lighthouse, surrounded by a crisp white border, would draw attention for its eye-catching boldness and its simplicity. The copy would be light, the signature stylized.

The firm's previous advertising had been largely small space placements, visually dominated by the rates the investment products paid and run in local newspapers. This new campaign was purely an image campaign, launched with four-color spreads and single pages in national business and news magazines—such as *Fortune, Business Week, Newsweek, U.S. News & World Report,* and

The New Yorker. It's focus was pure image: get the Van Kampen Merritt name and logo better known. The second ad showed the same lighthouse from a different perspective and carried the single word headline "Vigilance." The third, "Vision." Each ad, in brief copy, told of the concern of anxious investors and of the qualities that made them feel safer and more secure, made them *feel good* about their investment decisions—*Direction, Vigilance, Vision*—all part of a reassuring program of "Investing with a Sense of Direction."

Eight months into the campaign, research indicated recognition of the Van Kampen Merritt name had increased. Four times as many respondents claimed familiarity with the firm and its lighthouse symbol. Further, the tone of the marketing effort improved, as did morale overall among the firm's several hundred employees, who *felt good* seeing their firm presented so visibly and vividly.

Image advertising is, after all, *feel good* advertising.

The campaign won awards but, more importantly, it gained sales.

One year after the second round of research, Van Kampen Merritt was still increasing its level of awareness, while its leading competitors' levels of recognition were flat. The firm recognized it had a longer way to go . . . and was, indeed, *going*. Brokers want to sell products their clients know and to which they are receptive. The purpose of the steady, high-visibility campaign in national media was to tell brokers and their clients that Van Kampen Merritt was a "presence" in the industry.

They felt that presence.

Some Campaigns That Didn't Quite Work

Fast food is about as competitive as any industry in existence. Category leader McDonald's is a success story virtually unmatched—not that competitors haven't tried.

When Wendy's succeeds with such good-humored messages as "Where's the Beef?" it momentarily makes Big
Mac look pompous and institutional. Burger King, too,
tries very, very hard—sometimes too hard. In an attempt
to be hip and funny, Burger King's $40-million, 1986 cam-
paign built around "Herb the Nerd"—the man who never
ate a Burger King Whopper, totally lost sight of the purpose of Burger King advertising: to sell hamburgers. By
creating an unlikable character (about whom no one even
remotely cared) and putting him in a series of commercials that had nothing to do with the product or its benefits, the advertiser and its agency not only didn't win approval and sales, it annoyed and insulted its audience.
Herb vanished from view after four months, yet four
years later, the advertising industry still refered to it as
one of the most embarrassing ad campaigns of the 1980s.
Again guilty of trying too hard, Burger King's sequel
campaign—"We do it like you'd do it when we do it like
we do it at Burger King"—had as it's only redeeming
quality the absence of Herb the Nerd. The company had
veered a long way from its early, simple theme, "Have it
your way at Burger King."

Few companies enjoy the status of Sears Roebuck &
Company, that of a *bona fide* household name. For generations Sears was the place America shopped for back-to-
school clothes, bedspreads and linens, and all major ap-
pliances.

You could trust Sears.

They were always moderately priced—not the cheap-
est, not the most expensive.

And there was that Sears guarantee, whether it was
your car battery or the elastic in your socks: if it wasn't
right, take it back to any Sears store and a friendly person
from the neighborhood would make everything right.

Sears was truly "Where America Shopped". . . until
America was distracted by a blue light special.

K-Mart, the offshoot of S.S. Kresge (historically
America's runner-up five-and-dime store), suddenly (or

so it seemed) had covered the nation with large, well-lit stores with plenty of free parking and adequate-quality merchandise at heavily discounted prices. Sears became where America shopped when it couldn't find what it wanted at K-Mart or Wal-Mart or one of the number of merchandise barns that sprouted as anchors of the shopping malls of the 1970s.

Sears' problems as a retailer were not unique—only bigger. They had more locations, so they suffered the shoppers' exodus in larger numbers. Further, the company had made a major move to diversify by using its Allstate Insurance subsidiary as a component of the highly touted Sears Financial Network, adding acquisitions Coldwell Banker and Dean Witter for real estate and investment brokerage respectively. America's store now offered, it was said, everything you wanted from stocks to socks.

The Sears Financial Network was a huge disappointment. The company's masterplan failed to take into account changes in lifestyles, particularly among the lower-income, value-oriented shopper and the much-desired baby boomers. Sears' strengths were that it would offer easy credit and it was in the neighborhood. The shopper of the 1970s was more mobile by inclination and orientation. The automobile made shopping outside the community easier and the large parking lots of the malls and stores of the suburbs—serving a much larger community—were inviting. The bank charge cards, especially Mastercard and Visa, made credit available in stores previously off-limits. And one-stop shopping was a less attractive convenience to "the boomers" who were willing to travel large distances and check out other stores, preferring specialties over "department store real estate agents and stock brokers."

But as late as Sears management was to recognize its miscalculations, its (and its ad agency's) response was no less ill-conceived. At a time when the country was being swept with buzz-words, computer language, and trendiness, Sears based its comeback attempt around an ad campaign under the banner "Everyday Low Prices." The very phrase had a 1950s ring in the high-tech 1980s. In addition, the perception it created was if Sears had to reposition itself with "Everyday Low Prices," that must mean Sears believed its prices had been too high consistantly and that was why it lost market share. The general perception was that Sears' prices weren't the problem, but that the retailer had not kept pace with the times. Their clothing line was considered unstylish by virtually all standards and they lagged behind on simple conveniences, such as suburban locations and parking facilities.

And if the motto "Everyday Low Prices" was not bland enough, Sears countered competition Montgomery Ward's trendy appliance department "Electric Avenue" with "Sears' Brand Name Central." The labeling and positioning were so lacking in style as to be dismissed as boring.

Once again, the company failed to take the pulse of its constituents. Times had changed, styles had changed, and Sears decided to take the gloves off and go after the competition with what sounded like a thirty-five year-old positioning statement. The lack of style and benefits to the consumer caused the costly re-launch of America's largest store to fizzle.

*   *   *   *   *

Bill Cosby is one of the most successful entertainers in the world. A veteran of at least three successful network TV series, numerous hit films, record albums, concerts and the author of several best-selling books, Mr. Cosby is naturally a much sought-after commercial spokesman. Few are better at it. His great strength is his obvious affection for children. Cosby and kids sold together perfectly. In a series of television spots for the various Jell-O products, Mr. Cosby with children entertained and moved enormous quantities of desserts. Even without children, his work for Ford, Coke, and Kodak is stylish, memorable, and effective. With his high public approval rating and phenomenally successful track record as a commercial spokesman, few questioned the wisdom of his selection as spokesman for the investment company, E.F. Hutton. Apart from the fact that the company was in a public relations and legal mess, having been charged with check-kiting, the Cosby signing totally backfired.

He should have provided warmth and public approval. Instead the man who made people laugh stood serious—even solemn—when he said how much he trusted E.F. Hutton. The man who teased and tickled children, to the delight of viewers stood stone-faced in a dark business suit. He wasn't funny. He wasn't warm. He was a *paid spokesman*. The general public, too, assumed that a person of Mr. Cosby's immense wealth maintained a company of lawyers and business managers to tend his investments. So he was also *not believable*—perhaps the first requirement of a celebrity presenter. The company hired Bill Cosby to make it seem less institutional, less cold and calculating. But Mr. Cosby was not then allowed to *be* Mr. Cosby. He was just another spokesman in a suit—except more expensive.

To review and summarize:

1 Recognize that no one should be permitted to do anyone else's job. Writers write, research analysts analyze and artists contribute their talents in design, color and visual strength. Administrators—managers—should motivate, support and encourage. Demand that the work stay on track and on budget, but let others do their job.

2 Everyone knows what they like, what works for them, but not everyone is an expert when it comes to creating advertising or knowing what works for others. Use research; don't dictate personal tastes.

3   Require that lawyers limit their participation to the extent of advising what is and isn't *legal*.

4   If you use a celebrity presenter, be sure he or she is someone who is believable, loyal and won't overshadow your product.

5   Don't accept an agency recommendation that looks obviously like "a campaign in search of a product." The best advertising begins with the product's benefits to the customer. The creative "big idea" grows out of that.

6   Keep the number of players in the process small. When the CEO and the treasurer begin writing and directing, it's not just the agency that has a problem.

7   Communicate with your agency. That means both *talk* and *listen*. Don't let the opinion of the CEO's wife or husband outweigh the agency recommendation based on research and experience.

8   Set benchmarkers for success. Pre-test, test and qualify the results of your advertising.

9   Keep minutes of all meetings. People remember things differently.

10   "Dare to be different" doesn't mean go over the edge just for the *sake* of being different. It means be unique and creative, while being mature and professional. Remember, advertising should be exciting and stimulating, but it is also a business with a purpose.

Media

As is the case with research, media planning and coordination are key components of successful advertising. Like research it is not easy to place these components sequentially in the advertising process. Media like research must be considered throughout the market research, strategy and creative development stages, just as research should be conducted before creative work begins, continue as part of creative development and fine-tuning and as a monitoring device during the run of the campaign and, finally, as a tool for evaluating your success (or lack thereof). Media decisions hover over most phases of your campaign development.

From the moment you first develop or are presented with your advertising budget, you must begin projecting, considering or ruling out media. Can you afford television? Can there be a strong mix of media throughout the year or will the budget dictate "flights"—concentrated periods of activity with layoffs in between? Can you afford to run a national program or will lack of dollars force a concentrated regional campaign? Or multi-region? Which media works best in your targeted regions? What of demographics? What, if any, is the media of choice of our target audience?

169

Some early media decisions influence creative development. For example, if you expect to advertise in *The New Yorker*, the tone of your creative would be different from an ad you would place in *TV Guide*. *Vanity Fair* does not provide the same advertising environment as *People* magazine even though you may be targeting an individual who reads both magazines—or all four magazines mentioned. The creative team must be aware of not only the strategy of the campaign, but also the environment for the ads they create. Daytime soap operas, late news or cable comedy shows may have the same viewers, but each occupies a very different environment. The same commercial spot may be jarringly out of place in different programs. The client's role in these decisions should be to attend the strategy meeting and then relax. Just as a CEO should not get bogged down writing copy, a CEO should not sit debating *TV Guide* or *Parade*.

For an ad to work, it must be seen. The poorly written mimeographed handbill (misspellings and all) taped to the street lamp at the bus stop gets attention. It may be for a political candidate, a garage sale, a lost dog or a retailer going out of business, but it's an *ad*. Of the people standing and waiting for a bus at the corner *nearly everyone* is likely to look at such a posted handbill and read at least a part of it. As much cannot be said for every ad in the newspaper that same day. Nor would the audience see or hear every television and radio spot to which they were exposed.

What is the cost differential between a mimeographed handbill and thirty seconds of network TV time?

Substantial.

This is not a recommendation that clients and agencies concentrate on the mimeographed handbill market to the exclusion of other advertising media. It *is* however, a recommendation that you not overlook the obvious. Big isn't always better. Television, radio, direct mail, outdoor advertising, telemarketing, out-of-home (cab interiors, public transit terminals, etc.), co-oped sides of the wrappers of other products, in-flight, point of sale—even shop-ping cart advertising—all have a specific impact and influence. To take our best shot at getting the consumer's attention doesn't always mean taking the big or glamorous route. Television reaches the largest audience, usually costs the most and in most instances proves to be the best vehicle for generating a high level of awareness and influence—fast.

The two most relevant words to media directors are *reach* and *frequency*: how many prospects can we reach and how often can we reach them with the available budget? Yet, sometime maximum numbers are not as important as the *right* numbers. Presumably everyone is a target prospect for a toothpaste ad, so nearly every media option may be considered—*Time* magazine, an airport billboard, rock radio, talk radio, cable's Weather channel, *60 Minutes* or the 1,000th rerun of *I Love Lucy*. That's *toothpaste*. But what of, say, Jaguar automobiles? Is a television program with an audience largely composed of teenagers, middle income homemakers, or retirees living on a fixed income the best media option? Is a billboard or transit sign in a lower income community the best placement—or even an acceptable placement—for a luxury car ad? Of course not.

The television show *thirtysomething* is a big hit, although it's never in the handful of top-rated shows and rarely even wins its time slot in the ratings. It is a hit because the audience it *does* attract are of an age, income and lifestyle that represent prospects who are highly desirable to advertisers: twenty-five to forty-four years old; middle-upper middle income; educated; urban. These people buy disposable convenience products and luxury items; go to movies; buy stereo equipment, drink wine and follow fashion trends. So to reach a significant number of *them* is more important than reaching a large number of persons who are *not* prospective users of such products.

Your research has defined the prospects for your product and told you some things about them, such as how much, if any, television they watch and what, if any, newspapers and magazines they read. What else?

Because every ad must be seen or heard, let's consider some options:

1. Newspapers
   a. daily (including Sunday)
   b. weekly
   c. local (city or community)
   d. national
   e. trade or specialty
2. Magazines
   a. consumer or general interest
   b. business
   c. trade
   d. specialty or sponsored

3. Television
   a. network
   b. local
   c. cable
   d. satellite
4. Radio
5. Outdoor (billboards)
6. Out-of-home
   a. transit
   b. shelter
   c. point-of-sale
   d. posters, signage
7. Direct Mail
8. Others

a. in-flight
b. video
c. packaging
d. promotion items and novelties

Newspapers

Not too many years ago newspapers were being termed an endangered species. Across the United States, papers with long, distinguished histories, as well as well-financed, heavily promoted new ventures, were failing at a rapid clip. Union contracts, paper shortages, tough competition from other media and shrinking corporate ad budgets all conspired to make the local newspaper seem destined to go the way of the family farm and the horse and buggy.

Then everything changed. Some termed it merely a shakeout process. Some newspapers were bought by national or international media companies and took on new life. Whatever the reason, the newspaper in America is alive and well and still the daily habit of millions. Research indicates newspaper readers tend to be older, the largest segment in the fifty-five to sixty-four age range. More than just reporting news and community happenings, the modern newspaper puts a greater emphasis on lifestyle. Sports and entertainment sections are more involving and less detached. The greatest values of newspapers to advertisers are habit and immediacy. They are timely and familiar. Both daily and weekly papers are reflective of the market. The ad that shows the picture and copy, while allowing for rereading and viewing, still is the current edition and the ad material is as fresh and timely as the news that surrounds it. Thus, such headlines as "Grand Opening," or "Hurry! Last Two Days of Our Giant Sale!," take on freshness other print media can't always provide.

While people feel a connection to their hometown papers, loyal readers tend to embrace national offerings such as *The Wall Street Journal, USA Today, Investors Daily* and numerous trade and specialty papers—*Daily Variety* and *Women's Wear Daily* are just two of the more influential.

Magazines

General interest magazines include the major news weeklies *Time, Newsweek,* and *U.S. News & World Report* and other majors such as *Life, People, The New Yorker* and *TV Guide.* Advertising in these magazines may be purchased on a national or regional basis, in four-color process or black and white, and in a range of sizes from column inches to gatefold. Magazines as a choice of media allow for both a selectivity of reader as well as a predictable environment. While you may not be sure of the story or article nearest your ad in the daily paper, you can be reasonably certain of the tone of the material in *Business Week, Fortune, Forbes* or *Rolling Stone.* The range of possibilities is nearly endless. In addition to the special focus of the magazines mentioned, titles ranging from *Sports Illustrated, Tennis* and *Golf* to *Popular Photography, Motor Trend* and *Brides* enable you to target your ad message more narrowly than ever before to large market segments.

The dominant market segment for magazine readership appears to be the highly desirable advertiser target, the "baby boomer," aged twenty-five to forty-four. Consider: today's magazine buyer is willing to pay cover prices of $3, $4 or $5 for a single issue for information and entertainment, knowing full well that perhaps 50 percent of the magazine's content will be advertising. Over recent years, a growing number of magazines (*Rolling Stone, Town & Country, Vogue, Harper's,* to name a few) are being purchased as much for the advertising as for the editorial. There is an increasing status-consciousness attached to being an advertiser in certain trendsetting magazines. The creative content of the ads is every bit (or more) as memorable and creative as many of the features. To a significant percentage of people, buying or subscribing to a magazine is a statement of their lifestyle (*New Republic, Playboy, The New Yorker, Spy, GQ, Cosmopolitan*), and the advertisers in those magazines become participants in the lives the readers live or to which they aspire. Unlike newspapers, magazines may *attempt* timeliness, but maintain lengthy lead times, ranging from weeks to months, for both articles and ads.

Increasingly, specialty magazines are appearing which are largely subsidized by a single advertiser. Such titles as *Philip Morris* magazine and Fidelity Investments' *Investment Vision* seek to provide the look and tone of popular consumer magazines, while co-opting the content and attempting to influence readers through editorial as well as ad pages. If budgets permit publishing magazines of the quality of the two noted, the results can be tremendous in terms of building brand loyalty influencing various targeted groups such as regulators, legislators and industry members, as well as consumers.

Television

As noted, television has long been acknowledged as the medium by which advertisers can reach and influence the largest numbers of people in the shortest time. It has also been regarded as the most costly medium and, as such, unaffordable to most advertisers.

Not anymore.

Television may be as competitively affordable as other media, while also offering the ability to target an audience segment as precisely as its print and direct mail competition. Clients often shift uneasily when agencies mention TV, thinking the agencies prefer TV as a glamorous medium, but it is too broad, too big for most modest ad budgets. That's not true either. Once the choice to TV advertisers was between network and local and the range of programming was equally limiting. As TV looked for high ratings, it sought the largest audience for its shows, concentrating on comedy, variety or dramatic programming with mass appeal. This type of programming meant both high cost and considerable "waste"—viewers who were not prospective customers.

Television today offers as many options and alternatives for programming as a newsstand does for magazines. In addition to the three major networks, ABC, CBS and NBC, and Fox Television, most cities have one or several local independent VHF and UHF stations, offering alternative programs at much lower ad rates, reflective of the smaller projected audiences.

But the major revolution came with the arrival of cable television. Cable is not only *more* television and to many, *better* television, but *targeted* television. While movies and concerts on HBO and Showtime get the publicity and become synonymous with cable in the public consciousness, a typical system will carry some sixty channels, offering the broadest range of programming from opera to science to sports. Opportunities for advertisers lie in targeting commercials to the demographic group matching prospects to cable channels—*FNN* (Financial News Network), *CNN* (Cable News Network), *Lifetime* (women-oriented programming), *BET*, (Black Entertainment Television), *The Discovery Channel* (science and nature programming) and many more, including Spanish language, health and sports programming. Many of the advertising opportunities are available on a regional or city basis. Nationally, ad rates are competitive with national magazines and, most importantly, the specialized programming means a better-defined audience. Viewers of the Financial News Network, for example, expect to see commercials for financial products (mutual funds, brokerage firms, other investment-oriented spots). Sportschannel's audience is receptive to commercials aimed at their interests and lifestyle. Waste is minimal. Baby boomers have VH-1, country music fans have *The Nashville Network*; and *Nickelodeon* is for the kids.

Some cable and UHF channels have come under fire for airing sponsored programs that have the look and tone of familiar format shows but are, in effect, full program-length ad presentations. Nutrition products, weight-loss plans, real estate investing companies and skin care companies have used this format. Satellite programs are not at all controversial and are presented similar to the format of closed circuit seminar broadcasts. Program content is identified as being presented by and for a clearly defined group. A sixty-second commercial can convey a lot of information. Thirty second commercials are still the most common, but some TV will accept fifteen-or even ten-second spots.

Radio

As an advertising medium, television emphasizes its visual benefits—people can see the product, what it can do, the color of its packaging, its logo and so on. Radio ad reps are not intimidated by this argument. They point out that radio listeners tend to be, as a group, more loyal and consistent. They think of radio personalities as their friends. They wear T-shirts with their station's call letters. They'll call in to chat on or off the air. Even without the call, radio is a "closer" medium, with the announcer or disc jockey having a conversation with listeners in their homes, offices and cars, without the "barrier" of a screen.

Sound persuasive? We haven't even discussed the "theatre of the mind" argument. In *Advertising Theory and Practice*, Dr. C. H. Sandage and Dr. Vernon Fryburger note; "all advertising media have some limitations. The life of a radio or television advertisement is no longer than the time it takes for presentation. If an announcement is broadcast at a time when few prospects are listening, it is lost forever so far as most prospects are concerned, unless carried on by word-of-mouth publicity occasioned by listeners or viewers . . . In addition, two out of every three listeners to the radio engage in some other activity while the radio is on."

Bob Schulberg of CBS Radio counters in his 1989 book, *Radio Advertising*: "Listeners are loyal and friendly and, in many cases, harbor true familial feelings toward the stations they listen to. But if a radio station is not satisfying its public, listeners do not turn off the radio. They turn to another station." Like TV, radio's costs are based on ratings—who has the largest audience in the various time frames. Like the magazine, radio is specialized, targeted, station formats aimed at a particular audience—youth, news-hungry, sports-minded, highbrow or nostalgia buff. Research from 1988 indicates that more than half of all radio listening takes place outside of the home—in cars, in public places, in offices and with the advent of personal radios and headsets, anywhere a listener wants to go. This clearly shows radio is not limited to the single "wake-up call" of a generation ago.

Outdoor

Outdoor advertising used to be called simply "billboards." That was back when telemarketing was called "phone soliciting." The most common outdoor ad for many years was the twenty-four-sheet poster. Today, technology has made a wide variety of sizes and techniques available, along with extensions and mechanical devices, creating smoke, moving parts, three-dimensional effects and reflective lights. Many advertisers were wary of outdoor boards as weather had its effect and colors would fade, run or both. Today, the most finely detailed photograph can be reproduced on a board and withstand the elements adequately. As with a retail business, the key to a successful outdoor ad can be summed up in three words: location, location, and location. We began this section by saying that in order to work, an ad must be seen. Certainly, that is nowhere more true than in outdoor advertising. The right location, however, can be powerfully effective in creating or increasing the level of awareness that leads to sales.

Out-of-home

Once out-of-home advertising and billboards were the same thing. Today, out-of-home is as specialized as any form of advertising. It may include signs on sides of buses, on roofs of cars and taxis, at bus shelters, train stations, in elevators or lobbies, on theatre marquees, airlines, in public buildings, in phone booths, in a plaza—even on restroom walls. Anywhere there's a space, there's an opportunity for a message. If someone paid to put it there, it's an ad.

Direct Mail

Although listed seventh among media alternatives, direct mail is historically a first choice among many advertisers. Nearly half of the American adult population has responded to a direct mail offer. *What* to mail is nearly limitless in terms of creativity and functionality. Here, again, research is essential. One person's valuable mail is another's junk mail. To some, a catalog, credit card, brochure, invitation, newsletter, booklet, magazine, coupon, order form, price list, calendar or *poster* is a treasure; to others it is unwanted and irrelevant. To both, it can be expensive. Choose carefully who receives your mailing.

Direct mailers accept as the most basic of rules that *the list is everything*. It is your audience; just as the readers of a magazine or viewers of a TV program are your target group, the names on your list had better comprise the most receptive audience for your message or the effort is a waste. The format and content of a mailing can be as simple and relatively inexpensive as a card or a letter; or it can be as costly as the production of a TV commercial—and just as creative, with anything from a book to a record or multi-part, four-color presentation.

U.S. Media Billings by Category

Media	Top 25 agencies 1988 billings	as % of top 500	Top 100 agencies 1988 billings	as % of top 500	Top 500 agencies 1988 billings
Print					
Newspaper	$1,406	43.8	$2,403	74.7	$3,214
Consumer magazine	2,785	63.0	3,688	83.4	4,421
Sunday magazine	17	26.3	42	65.6	63
Business publications	351	35.0	624	62.0	1,005
Medical journal	118	25.0	310	65.7	472
Farm publication	1	2.2	34	54.1	62
Broadcast					
Spot TV	4,352	59.4	6,098	83.2	7,325
Network TV	8,192	84.1	9,340	95.8	9,742
Cable TV	377	61.0	558	90.3	617
Syndicated TV	229	77.6	271	91.8	295
Radio	1,220	54.4	1,740	77.6	2,241
Other					
Outdoor	382	61.4	516	82.7	623
Other*	2,744	56.3	3,724	76.4	4,871

Notes: Dollars are in millions. Information in this chart is compiled from media breakouts supplied by 460 of the top 500 agencies reporting $35 billion in media billings. *Other includes billings from free-standing inserts, transit ads, point of sale, direct response, sales promotion, special events and Yellow Pages. AA will publish a ranking of sales promotion agencies May 1, 1989 and a ranking of direct response agencies May 15, 1989.

Media as % of $35 billion in billings

Other: 13.9%
Newspaper: 9.2%
Consumer magazine: 12.6%
Radio: 6.4%
Synd. TV: 0.8%
Cable TV: 1.8%
Network TV: 27.9%
Spot TV: 21.0%
Sunday mag: 0.2%
Business pubs: 2.9%
Medical journal: 1.3%
Farm publication: 0.2%
Outdoor: 1.8%

AA chart: Kevin Brown

Advertising Age, March 29, 1989. Courtesy of Crain Communications, Inc.

NEWSPAPER
A U D I E N C E

People aged 35 to 64 are more likely to buy newspapers, according to the Consumer Expenditure Survey. Newspaper readership should expand because of the aging of the baby boom.

(percent of householders who buy newspapers, by age of householder)

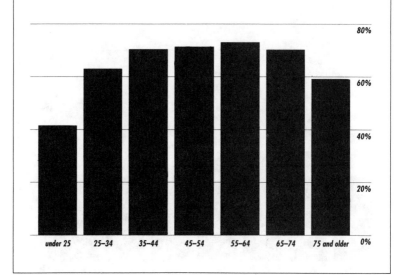

Source: 1986 Consumer Expenditures Survey, Bureau of Labor Statistics.
© *American Demographics. Reprinted with permission.*

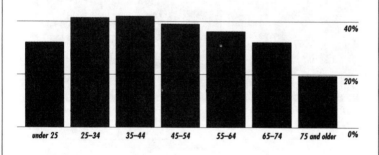

THE
MAGAZINE
A U D I E N C E

People aged 25 to 54 are most likely to buy magazines. With the baby-boom generation filling this middle-aged group, the 1990s could be the golden age for magazines, but only if magazines target their specific niches and needs.

(percent of householders who buy magazines, by age of householder)

under 25	25–34	35–44	45–54	55–64	65–74	75 and older	

100%
80%
60%
40%
20%
0%

Source: 1986 Consumer Expenditures Survey, Bureau of Labor Statistics.
© *American Demographics. Reprinted with permission.*

THE TELEVISION
A U D I E N C E

In nearly every time slot, people aged 55 and older are more likely to be watching television than younger people. This is good news for the television industry, as the generation raised on television ages.

(percent of people watching television, by age and time slot, weekdays only, 1988)

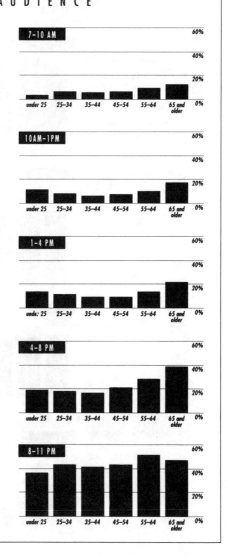

Source: Multimedia Audiences Report, Spring 1988, Mediamark Research, Inc.
© American Demographics. Reprinted with permission.

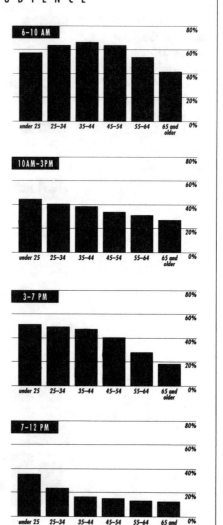

THE
RADIO
A U D I E N C E

Except for drive-time hours (6–10 a.m.), younger people are more likely than older adults to listen to radio. More programming geared to older listeners, such as all-news formats, may turn these statistics around.

(percent of people listening to radio, by age and time slot, weekdays only, 1988)

Source: Multimedia Audiences Report, Spring 1988, Mediamark Research, Inc.
© American Demographics. Reprinted with permission.

There are a number of sources for qualified lists: your own current or inactive customers; lists rented from brokers; lists purchased from list companies; lists rented or purchased from publications serving your industry; or lists traded or exchanged with others (such as an auto dealer offering a list to a company selling car stereos or seat covers in exchange for a fee or a list of *their* customers for solicitation by the dealer's service department).

Entire volumes are written on this aspect of advertising alone. It is every bit as specialized as TV or print production and highly effective. Some agencies handle *only* direct mail clients. It's flexible, confidential, manageable and can be very cost-effective.

Others

In-flight movies now usually open with a commercial. (Sometimes it's done subtly, such as an ad for the airline itself, noting its various routes and discounts or club benefits.)

The *sides of packages* of various products may carry a sales promotion (contest or other offer) which is, in effect, an ad.

Video cassettes, sold or rented, initially contained only the video production itself, then trailers (previews of other videos) were added, and later actual commercials. A survey of viewers revealed their intention was to "fast forward" through the advertising. This is where the challenge comes in. If the commercial is entertaining or informative—simply, *creative*—enough, people will watch. Once America claimed it got up and left the room when the commercials came on. Now they often find the commercials more entertaining then some of the programs.

In-theatre ads are controversial. People resent paying an admission to a movie and then having to sit through advertising. Research has shown, however, as with videocassettes, if the spot is creative enough people will not only watch without complaint, they will respond.

Give-away items that are often part of a sales promotion effort are sometimes independent and are advertisements by another name: pens, key rings, shopping bags and umbrellas are all ads if they carry a name and/or logo.

Perhaps the most amazingly successful example of well-executed advertising is in the market for fashion at all levels. There was a time not long ago when companies gave away t-shirts, sweat shirts, caps and head bands with their names and logos as promotional gifts. The give-aways were, in effect, payment to people who walked around advertising their product or company. Today logos are a fashion statement. Clothing and department stores sell thousands of shirts, jackets and caps with radio station logos. TV networks have opened shops where the public can buy clothing and items not just promoting favorite shows, but the networks themselves. People are paying to walk the streets and beaches wearing an NBC or CBS logo. Coca Cola has an enormously successful line of clothing, as does McDonald's.

Still another example is the *card* in a magazine that is sometimes called a "blow-in" or a "tip-in" or is bound-in. It is an ad for *another* ad which is usually on the page of the magazine which follows the card. The card contains an abbreviated version of the ad's message and is a response mechanism ("Please enter my subscription at this amazing low price," or "Yes! Send me my free Melrose Park street map just for looking at the Amazing Whizzbanger in my home for 10 days!").

The postage-paid card is a great device. It increases response rate significantly. People hate having to hunt for a stamp *besides* writing in all the information requested. So it's additional promotion for the advertiser, a convenience to the customer/reader, a response-enhancer and a consumer postage-saver.

It is also too much of a good thing. The average magazine now has five to seven such cards intruding on the magazine reader. Here's the problem: people have always liked to "skim" all or parts of magazines. Thumb poised, they would flip through the pages, back to front, then front to back. But all those bound-in cards keep people from flipping through the pages. One advantage of this to advertisers is that skimmers were exposed to ads that they would otherwise not see if they only turned to specific articles or columns on the pages listed in the table of contents. An argument in favor of the card is that an intrusion which stops the reader at that page, *forces* the reader to see the ad. However, if the reader *resents* being stopped at the page, the mindset at the time of exposure to the ad may be negative. Further, advertisers who *do not* have a card intruding at their page get "skimmed over" as the magazine falls open to someone else's ad. Research says that an increasing number of persons now rip out the response cards before flipping through a magazine. This not only negates the purpose of the card, but wastes advertisers' money, as the cards are media costs over and above that of the ad page. When the cards are for subscription offers from the publication itself, (which is all too often) the intrusion becomes an even greater nuisance. The typical magazine now includes three subscription solicitation cards per issue.

Some publications will tell an advertiser, "We'll put one of our subscription cards in front of your ad so the book will automatically fall open to your page."

Note to magazine: Don't do us any favors! If the reader resents the intrusion of the card, how will they feel about being "forced" to look at our ad? Further, the cards are *helpful* to people responding, but again research notes that, when given a choice between a coupon (card) or an 800-number, more than 95 percent of persons responding use the phone.

As noted in the "Creative" section of this book, media is an area rich in diverse opinions. Most people have a favorite TV show, magazine, radio station—even, perhaps a firm conviction that a certain bridge into the city is the only possible place a billboard can be effective.

Listen to your research. Your favorite show may be great entertainment, but you've hired an agency to create terrific ads that will sell your product. Don't insist they only travel in circles which you frequent yourself.

Considering that there are thousands of media options available, again, let the agency do its job by evaluating and recommending the best fit. Most mid-size to large agencies (even some small ones) have media data on their computers. Those that don't most likely rely on the library of *Standard Rate and Data* directories. The agency that buys only what you request may be good at taking orders, but are they as good as you can hire at buying media?

Clients should accept the media representative's invitations to luncheons and presentations. It's important that clients know what's going on in media firsthand. But remember, the agency works for *you* and is expected to review *your* full range of media options and negotiate the best possible deals. If a media rep knows or believes that you are eager to do business and/or that your order is "in the bag," you will have not only undermined your agency's status with the media, but reduced your own chances of making the best possible deal. Like so much else, competition in media is intense. Today, more than ever before, creative merchandising options and frequency deals are possible under much more favorable terms—if you know how to get them.

Sometimes the use of a media consultant or a media buying service can prove tremendously cost-effective. For example, a smaller agency looking to make the best spot market buys around the country, will know when to call up the reserves. Media buying services should cost the client no more and will often provide lower costs on larger, more complicated buys. Through a variety of methods (buying "remnants"—unsold broadcast time and print space at a discount and re-selling it to its clients or buying large blocks of time at a volume discount and re-selling it to clients) a buying service can work with your small agency to provide big agency services. They can also work with bigger agencies in complex or regional media plans to produce substantial savings.

In many respects, a media service is like a travel agent, experienced in dealing with media on both a local and global level. They are privy to opportunities that may develop suddenly, such as large cancellations of media time or space that may be acquired at huge discounts.

The term "clout" is used often in media and has the same meaning as it does in politics: power. Most agencies, large and small, claim to have it. It's virtually a requirement for the job. In fact, most agencies *can* have it, if they understand the mechanics of their business. In buying media for a very large client, clout is a built-in feature. Recognize it. Like the auto dealer who insists he needs $10,000 but will bar the door upon learning you've got $8,100 cash in your pocket, media people know they must be flexible. The top-rated TV shows don't negotiate ad rates *much*, but even they negotiate. Much of the industry believes clients who "pay the rate card" are being ill-served. Usually, a talented media buyer will maximize the buying power of both the large *and* the small budget.

"Value added" is a relatively recently coined phrase for the old practice of merchandising. Most media entities hate it—the same way agencies hate to do spec creative work and for the same reason—it means giving something away. In media it might mean bonus spots on radio or TV or extra copies of a magazine or a subsidized mailing or a premium position at no charge or a color ad for the cost of black and white. The possibilities are endless, as they should be. Your media buyer's job is to get the absolute maximum for your budget. That almost never means buying retail. Note the term *almost*. The law of supply and demand always applies. You can't buy what's already been taken, but if what you want is gone, that opens the door to an excellent opportunity to, say, buy second-best at the cost of third-best or possibly get third-best thrown in at a discount, too.

With all due respect, virtually all media reps have research that shows them beating the wind out of their competition. A skilled media planner knows not only how to read research, but how to read an *audit statement* and match it to the research. Skilled media planners and buyers and good media reps can form a partnership where everybody wins. The client's role should be to support an atmosphere that allows that to occur and to be a partner in it as well, not to interfere with it.

	Feb-May	June-Aug	Sep-Oct	Nov-Dec	Total
Corp. Image Ads	350,000	250,000	250,000	150,000	$1,000,000
Print	200,000	150,000	200,000	150,000	700,000
TV	150,000	100,000	50,000		300,000
Product Ads	150,000	250,000	500,000	500,000	$1,400,000
Print	100,000	200,000	365,000	400,000	1,065,000
TV	50,000		100,000	100,000	250,000
Direct Mail		50,000	35,000		85,000

At some point the budget, research, creative and media plan all come together after a series of intersections—each having influenced the other.

The media director needs to know how much he or she has to work with. The creative director needs some direction—how much TV, print, direct, other? The account executive needs to see a game plan of what will be done in what time frame and at what cost to assure accountability to the client. To begin shaping the plan, the account team meets. Research in hand, they know their product—*Good Life Insurance*, a new wholly-owned subsidiary of International Financial Services Corporation—and they have their research in hand. They know their target market is young savings/investment-oriented professionals, ages twenty-five to fifty. IFSC, the parent company, has told the agency the ad budget is $2.4 million for media, excluding production, and they have eleven months to generate some interest in *Good Life* and its products. He'd like to see $XX million business written that first year. The shareholders meeting is at the end of the calendar year.

The agency complains the budget is too small and the marketing vice president of *Good Life* says he doesn't have the personnel and other wherewithal to do the job properly and that's not nearly enough time. The CEO reminds everybody of the excellent employment opportunities in asbestos removal.

The game plan looks like this:

Objective: Introduce the company as an important new force in the industry.

Strategy: 1) Generate an awareness of the company's existence and its products, 2) Generate sales leads for brokers and salesmen.

Tactics: 1) Create and place television and print advertising in major and secondary media.

The budget breakout looks like this:

Image ads would introduce the name *Good Life* in major and secondary business and general interest magazines with a mix of color and black and white ads. The list would include such titles as *Fortune, Business Week, Forbes, Newsweek, U.S. News, Financial World,* and the *New York Times Magazine,* in a mix of national and selected regional editions. Television would include FNN and CNN, Cable TV.

Product ads would identify the specific insurance and investment products of *Good Life* and offer a brochure called "The Estate Planning Guide" free to those calling an 800-number in the ad or sending in a coupon in the ad's lower right-hand corner. TV ads will be a mix of thirty-second (image) and sixty-second (product) spots, both featuring the 800-number. Every placement will have a different extension number (or department number in the coupon address) to track the media as the source of the response.

Two direct mail drops will be made during the year. They will include a four-color announcement card—a *Good Life* image piece—a letter from the CEO of the parent company explaining why the world needed yet another insurance investment company and a postage-paid response card and envelope to be used in obtaining the free estate planning guide.

Had this been a real campaign instead of a hypothetical example, it would have been presented to the client by the agency account executive or supervisor, complete with the details; that is, the names of all print recommended, number of recommended placements in both black and white and color, the magazines' circulation and relevant demographic information, costs per insertion and totals. Any value-added data would be notèd. Comps would have been presented to show creative. A similar detailed breakout would show television day-parts, dates and cost per spot. Storyboards would show how the spots work. Similar comps of the direct mail would be presented along with a detailed explanation of the characteristics and qualities of the lists to be used.

However, since this is merely a hypothetical example, the summary should suffice. And since the whole thing is hypothetical, let's give it a happy ending: *Good Life Insurance* joined the ranks of industry leaders in its second year of operations; the marketing manager got a huge raise and a promotion; the agency won two Addys and a Clio and a budget increase of 500 percent.

Sales Promotions

The sales promotion firm D.L. Blair ran a full page ad in *Advertising Age* with the headline "Why should you run a promotion when 95% of your prospects will never respond?" Their answer was "A good customer promotion can and will create awareness, excitement, conversion and trial among a significant number of prospects."

The same trade journal ran a page one story in February 1989, with the headline "The Party's Over—Food giants pull back on marketing, but boost promotion." The story described firms such as Quaker Oats, Kraft, General Foods, Kellog's and Anhauser-Busch, among others, "favoring consumer and trade promotion at the expense of media advertising."

What is somewhat surprising is that sales promotion was long considered, like direct mail, simply a part of the advertising media mix. But like direct mail, it took on a life of its own, with consultants, budgets and even agencies engaged in it exclusively.

Promotions overlap and intersect to such a degree that while a sales promotion is a form of advertising, the most successful promotions have media advertising as an integral component. That is, promoting the promotion: four-color ads in magazines and Sunday newspapers and spots on TV and radio hype the sweepstakes or giveaway bonanza!

The sales promotion is a wonderful list-builder. A contest or sweepstakes that invites the public to write in and win a prize creates a mailing list of prospects that can be used, sold or both—often. A contest that goes the extra step and involves the public with such challenges as submitting an entry in the form of a recipe that uses your food product or a how-your-product-saved-the-day (made-me-laugh, saved-me-money, etc.) testimonial creates a file of information for the future. Cookbooks, prize winning essays, household tips . . . the possibilities go on and on.

A guarantee can become a promotion. Offering a money-back guarantee (or double your money back) creates another benefit to the consumer as a reason to buy as well as creating a sense of both quality and brand loyalty. Should the guarantee be utilized, you've earned a name for your mailing list and, ultimately, a satisfied customer and referrer who will endorse the integrity of your company.

Promotions that involve free samples usually lead to sales.

Discount coupons, two-for-one sales and offers of almost anything free or discounted leads to sales. Supermarkets offering tableware, towels, records, tapes, books, lawn chairs, dishes, pots and pans (buy one a week and collect the whole set, free or at discount with the purchase of $10, $20 of merchandise) are classics.

Agencies will (or should) offer to match up their clients in promotions by creating joint marketing campaigns. Some fall together naturally, such as airlines, hotels, car rentals and restaurants. Almost any combination of clients can work together with a bit of creativity. The result is an innovative offer and campaign and lower costs to the advertisers who share in the promotion.

An increasing number of advertisers are signing on as "sponsors" of events ranging from Little League and community sports to concerts and other productions. Chrysler, AT&T and American Express have been notable "sponsors" of Broadway and regional theatre productions. Visa sponsored Paul McCartney's world tour, Pepsi sponsored Michael Jackson and Budweiser sponsored the Rolling Stones. The benefit to the advertisers is their name on the marquee, tickets, program book, in all advertising and, often, right on stage in some form during the show. This leads to an identification with the subject to the audience for the event. Television programs such as the Bell Telephone Hour, the Voice of Firestone and Hallmark Hall of Fame were as much promotions as they were traditional media sponsorships, offering books, posters, records and other premiums to extend the reach of the tie-in.

To the enterprising advertising person, the field of promotions offers wide-open opportunities for visibility, good will, revenue, brand loyalty and sales. Among some of the most sought-after items are t-shirts bearing the *Motel 6* logo, caps with the *Batman* movie logo and *anything* with the name or likeness of the reigning pop star of the day...and your agency should be telling customers how to get one with the purchase of your products.

Philanthropy too can be a form of sales promotion: a client who creates an award (cash, scholarship, donation) named for itself basks in the goodwill that award creates. Warm feelings for the product follow close behind.

Service

There is a belief in advertising circles that an account is usually won on the basis of creative work and lost or retained because of service. Account service is the responsibility of "the suit," a term used sometimes with affection and other times in the way psychiatrists are called "shrinks" and police officers "cops." The suits are also, in many respects, the shrinks and cops of the agency/client relationship.

When an account executive is with a client, he or she is representing the agency—reflecting its creative talent, the experience, expertise, business sense and skills—and taking the heat when the client is displeased.

When the account exec is back at the agency, he or she is representing the client, responsible for the work staying on track and within budget, watching deadlines, coordinating research and media negotiations, plans and schedules. A good account exec is, in many respects, like a coach, supporting, motivating, prodding and (sometimes) screaming at the players to stay with the game plan, watch the clock and win the game. Account executives are professional communicators, often with a background in writing or producing, sometimes administration or media. On a normal day the creative department of the agency will grimace if "the suit" suggests a copy change or alteration in the layout. This is especially true in large agencies where "turf" is very defined. The first time the account exec says "It's a great idea, but it's not what the client asked for," or "The client will never buy that," or "I need it yesterday," the lines are drawn; the creative department asks "Whose side is this guy on?"

The answer is *the client's*.

If an account executive understands what the client needs and wants and exercises the discipline necessary to bring good work in on time, the agency should keep the client's business forever. Clients tend to forgive a creative approach that doesn't work. Lousy service is something else.

Early in this book we considered the choice of an ad agency and offered that it wasn't so much the size of the agency, but the people who comprise the account team that makes the difference—the *chemistry* of the participants. Advertising is, as are many others, a "people business." To be able to sell to people—to influence people through your advertising—you must understand them.

John O'Toole writes, "The advertising person who studies people as they really are, who is fascinated with what makes them do the things they do, who opens himself up to the rich and diverse society around him and applies what he learns there to his craft . . . this person is the most successful."

To succeed in advertising and keep the customer satisfied, the people on the agency team should be active listeners. The account exec should be the chief listener. But there are also times to be assertive. Among the pioneers and legends of advertising, as well as corporate leaders, probably the most often repeated piece of advice is to *let people do what they do best*. To *manage* or *direct* is not the same as to dominate or interfere.

Leaders *lead*. They don't trample their followers.

Robert McCourt, Director of Advertising and Sales Promotion, of American International Group, told *Business Month* magazine, "Agencies are too reactive. I think that it is incumbent upon somebody in my position to act as the centerpiece . . . and help define for the corporation what its needs and goals are."

Defining needs and goals—and making it all work—is the challenge that the client and agency must share. Here are some recommendations that help to define the account service relationship:

1   Meet with your agency at least weekly to review and fine-tune your program and be aware of developing opportunities or activities of competitors.

2   Alternate the site of the meetings. It is very healthy for the relationship to visit each other's offices frequently.

3   Make certain someone—agency or client—writes a meeting report, if only a brief summary. People remember things differently, and that can be very costly to all concerned.

4   Be certain you understand *why* you are using the media you are using. Too many corporate officers ask questions like "Why are we on cable?" or "Who reads *Inc.* or *Natural History* magazine?" Ad directors should never have to stammer or grope for an answer.

5   Share information with the agency on executive tastes. If someone likes classical music or modern art, personal tastes might be incorporated in creative work if it doesn't compromise the quality . . . or the point of the ad.

6   If the chemistry is wrong, ask for changes in the account team. Not everyone is compatible, and agencies would rather change account execs, creative or art directors or copywriters than lose an account or suffer an unhappy client (which is sometimes worse than losing an account).

7   *Be clear about what things cost.* It is unsettling for agencies to have their invoices questioned because you don't understand what you are paying for. Discuss a project's cost upfront.

8   *Exchange information.* Agencies should pass along columns or articles from trade publications or research reports; clients should share competive analysis or internal communications that may in any way affect the ad program.

9   *Define roles and protect each other.* When a client has a new personnel addition or change, that individual will often want to plug into the ad process without having an understanding of responsibilities and reporting relationships. A common question when a new player comes on is, "How will this affect us or our program?" Eliminate the anxiety by making clear who does what.

10   *Be ethical.* That may seem simple and obvious, but sometimes compromises are made without realizing it—a media junket or the innocent acceptance of a gift can be misread. Think and be careful.

Ethics

This last point bears some further consideration. Allan V. Palmer, Chairman of the Department of Marketing at the University of North Carolina at Charlotte, writes in the trade magazine *Marketing & Media Decisions* that "the evidence is increasingly abundant and persuasive that consumers, business executives, lawmakers, opinion leaders and marketers are becoming skeptical, cynical and dissatisfied with the ethical performance of marketing and advertising professionals."

Exhibit 7-1:   Advertisers Confidence in Agencies Ebbing

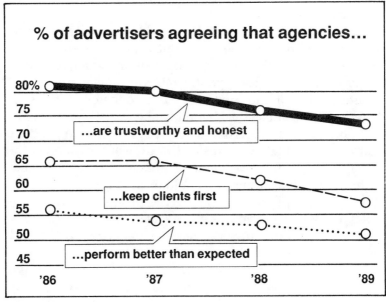

% of advertisers agreeing that agencies...

...are trustworthy and honest

...keep clients first

...perform better than expected

'86   '87   '88   '89

Source: Gallup Organization.

From *Advertising Age*, March 12, 1990. Courtesy of Crain Communications, Inc. Used with permission.

The motion picture *Crazy People,* a major Hollywood comedy, had as its premise an ad executive who believes in truth in advertising . . . so his employer has him committed to a mental institution.

In another film comedy, *How to Get Ahead in Advertising,* a brash young adman tells his wife "advertising is nothing more than a distortion of truth" that works only because people "want to believe something will work."

Financial World magazine devoted an entire issue to the subject of "Ethics in Business."

In 1989 the Speaker of the U.S. House of Representatives stepped down when his ethics came under fire and PBS ran an entire season of programs in which lawyers, writers, doctors, judges, politicians, journalists and an associate justice of the Supreme Court debated "Ethics in America." The subject is beyond timely . . . it's *fashionable.*

The claim is made that ad people exaggerate product claims to sell, that they mislead and airbrush, shoot film through filters and do whatever magic it takes to make nothing look like something. While there are unquestionably some people in advertising the profession would be better off without, we are a long way from the demons some find subliminally hiding in every haze, curl, cloud and puff of smoke.

Old joke: the devil says to the ad man, "I will make you rich and powerful beyond your wildest dreams in exchange for your soul and the souls of your wife and children." The ad man stares at him for a minute, then asks, "What's the catch?"

Advertising, perhaps more than most professions, seems to get a bad rap.

The usual assumption is that doctors go into medicine because of a calling to heal the sick and lawyers to law in a quest to see justice done. Any politician will gladly say with a straight face that public service is the honor and privilege of a dream come true. Wealth and power have nothing to do with the choice of a profession.

However, many folks believe advertising people will come up with a slogan, jingle or thirty-second spot for the devil himself if the budget's high enough. On the face of it, a pretty stupid, stereotypical opinion to hold, but sadly, one widely held. In most published surveys advertising people usually rank near the bottom in "Trust."

Do lawyers take cases defending people the whole world believes are guilty because they believe morality and the law require that *everyone* is entitled to representation? Or do they do it for a fee?

Upon learning of the huge, eight-figure sum Pepsi paid Michael Jackson to appear in their commercials, the world found it only interesting or amusing that the singer acknowledged openly he didn't use the product. Interesting and amusing, but not *unethical.*

Actress Cybill Shepherd was a national spokesperson for the beef council, though she often told interviewers she was a vegetarian. Unethical or just being a good capitalist?

What of the ethics of the ad execs who *put* them in these spots?

Many people in advertising have resigned accounts or have declined to work for clients whose position is the moral opposite of their own. Many agencies—large agencies with substantial overhead to support—will decline a cigarette account or a liquor account. Some will go as far as to issue public statements announcing their unwillingness to even *present* for such business. More than a few agencies have taken public positions on such issues as animal welfare, trumpeting their criticism of the fur industry's trapping and processing methods. In many instances this is viewed as opportunistic, exploitive—a not-so-subtle way of ingratiating themselves to a whole other tier of prospective clients who support the highly moral principles espoused. This might be viewed as a no-win situation: the ad agency is immoral and greedy if it accepts the business of a client whose product is somewhere between dubious and controversial. The same agency is just as suspect if it makes too public a gesture of distancing itself from said client. The definitive comment in this may simply be that you'll never be able to make some people happy no matter what you do.

In his highly regarded book *The Trouble with Advertising*, John O'Toole states, "The fact is that academicians, journalists, consumer advocates and government regulators criticize—and dislike—advertising because it isn't something else."

This is an interesting premise. As noted in our review of the pros and cons of "celebrity endorsements," many public figures, whether from the entertainment or public service fields, would never even consider a commercial endorsement because it was beneath them. Entire professions (accounting, medicine, legal, most types of consulting) considered it "undignified" to even advertise at all.

Yet, as Mr. O'Toole points out, while a recent poll showed that more the 80 percent of the respondents felt that "the claims for most products advertised on TV are exaggerated" and 52 percent said that most or all TV advertising is "seriously misleading," another study noted that 88 percent of those responding believed advertising is "essential" and "57 percent [said] advertising results in better products."

A simple and undisputed truth echoing throughout this book is that *advertising makes a product, service or business better known* and research study after study confirms that *better known products are perceived as better products.* With this perception, historically, has come the conclusion of a direct connection between level of awareness and share of market.

So is the conclusion that advertising is OK (maybe even *good*) but that *ad people* aren't? (Just as it's a good thing to be a nation of laws . . . if we could only do away with all the lawyers.)

Should we take comfort in the fact that ad people are in good company when lumped unfavorably with lawyers, politicians and religious fanatics?

Advertising is a service business, providing information to help people make more informed choices of the products and services they buy and use.

Advertising agencies provide a service to their clients, focusing, defining positions, showcasing, creating, merchandising with style, integrity . . . and ethics.

Martin Sorell, head of England's WPP Group—the company that owns both Ogilvy & Mather and J. Walter Thomson, among other agencies—told a convention audience that "in every other business I know, marketing strategy . . . commands huge [fees]. In the agency business, however, you give them away with the ads."

People in the ad business usually make a pretty decent living if they're good. They also give a lot away—money, counsel, service. And the really good ones avoid becoming full of themselves. That's part of the service too.

Budgets

Research, media and creative are the three most discussed, focused and debated components of advertising, but the budget is the factor that guides and limits—actually controls—everything. It *is* your operating plan and rules your marketing plan.

Typically, advertising budgets are determined far more arbitrarily than is admitted. Usually ad budgets are a percentage of the overall budget, but *what* percent is a reflection of how important advertising and promotion are to a client's top management. For clients who say ad budgets are determined by fixing a percentage of past sales, in a study of more than 2,000 clients using this rationale, the percentage ranged from an average of four tenths of one percent for insurance companies to an average of nearly 16.5 percent for makers of cosmetics.

Estimating the ad budget as a percent of *future* sales involves estimating and projecting the year ahead. Number crunchers and computers do this every year. Sometimes they "project" increases or losses, sometimes they forecast. They are usually conservative and unless the market for the product explodes, causing an unexpected move in either direction, they are usually pretty accurate.

The client whose position is "It doesn't matter how good a media or promotional opportunity is presented, that's all we've got to spend," is not technically correct. The issue is, what was *chosen* to spend? Just as hiring another person or reducing expenses in another department might be financed by the client reducing the ad budget (Heaven Forbid!), such decisions as *how much* or *what percent* are management decisions and judgement calls. If capital is allocated to cover operating expenses and advertising receives the remainder, it may be considered a budgeted amount, but it clearly has no relationship to what it takes to do the job.

Budgeting for advertising should be based upon the client's marketing plan. What are the objectives, the tactics to achieve these objectives and the cost to implement those tactics?

That sum is your ad budget.

If that amount cannot be committed, the marketing plan with its *objectives* must be revised. To reduce the budget when costs turn out to be simply more than was allocated dooms the plan to failure or demands that corners be cut. The result is not only "a thing without corners," it's bad advertising and bad business sense.

Compensation: Paying for Advertising

Agency compensation has always been a pretty touchy issue. Partly this is because we were brought up to believe it is impolite to talk about money. Advice from experts always seems to include the line ". . . and pay your agency fairly." Clients are inclined to say things like, "Of course we don't expect you to lose money on this account. We want to pay you fairly."

That word "fairly" is probably the problem. It's a relative term and relative terms are okay when they are comparing like quantities.

In hiring an ad agency, the client is entering into a *service* relationship and when a value is placed on a service it is most commonly determined on the basis of quality. Different levels of quality tend to go for different prices.

For years the formula was fairly simple: the agency received 15 percent of the media budget as commission. Large agencies only solicited clients with large budgets.

207

The volume of work performed on behalf of the large client seemed justified when big names appeared often in big places, and became a part of our culture.

The Marlboro man.
Does she or doesn't she?
The pause that refreshes.
You're in the Pepsi generation
You'll wonder where the yellow went . . .

Nobody seemed to complain to the industry that ads everyone recognized, for products everyone came to know, were costing too much. A campaign that failed to connect, however, was always described by how much it cost.

With smaller and medium-size accounts the media 15 percent commission may not amount to a fee that effects the true value of the ad program. For these clients, agencies work on a project basis, for a flat fee or on a fee basis, which sets a monthly amount for the agency's services; or on a combination of commission and fee.

The client has a budget and knows its ceiling amount. The agency has its overhead and is, in fact, in business to make a profit, so it knows what it needs to earn from an account to stay in business. In other professions the fee for services is stated outright. In advertising, its usually negotiated, quite defensively.

But not only is *talking* about money rude, The widely held image of advertising people is that their lifestyles are so, high—perhaps indulgent—as to make clients feel uncomfortable supporting them. Movie stars and athletes earn millions and flaunt it. Ad people earn far less, but are expected to behave and live in a modest fashion. Be creative, act creative—even a bit eccentric if you like, but don't flaunt it because it makes people think you're making too much money and doing so at their expense. And they resent it. As noted elsewhere in this book, in public (much less client) consciousness, advertising is not always accorded the status granted other professions, so not only is the initial compensation issue a sticky matter, but if budgets are cut, advertising is usually the first item to get the knife.

Part of this problem, incidentally, is of the agency business' own creation. It's a job people *choose* and often enjoy doing so much that there's a feeling that it shouldn't be fun and satisfying *and* pay well.

Richard Morgan wrote an *Adweek* column headlined "Terminal Insecurity: Why Agencies Don't Put Integrity Over Money." The headline says a lot, but the column makes a point agency/client relationships aren't as strong as they were. Once a client asked, "What can you do for me?" Today, the question is, "For how little can you do it?"

A number of consultants built lucrative practices for themselves by recommending very innovative—and complicated—compensation programs for agencies, tying agency income to such things as sales figures or research scores.

Proctor & Gamble has frequently been a standard setter in the business of advertising. In 1989, P & G developed a three-point agency payment system. In effect, it kept the basic 15 percent commission, but modified its payment structure to pay commissions for promotions that are, but not always categorized as, advertising. For products with very modest media budgets, P & G will pay a flat monthly fee. For its more substantially budgeted products if, at any time during the fiscal year, budgets are reduced, the agency will be compensated by a commission figure based on the original budget.

In their zeal to become global media superpowers, some agencies have made this process far more complicated than it ever needed to be.

A client has a budget, and the agency and client work on a plan of what can be realistically achieved within that budget. The agency will spend a certain amount of time on creative work, research, media planning and negotiating, production and service. An amount should be determined based on the scope of the job and prevailing competitive costs for such a job. Then factor in why this agency got the assignment rather than someone else. Considerations such as product industry experience and expertise (even reputation) have value over and above how cheaply it can be done.

At that point, whether it's paid as a monthly fee, billed at an hourly rate, or received through commissions becomes merely a function of accounting departments. Fair compensation is based on time and talent—any arrangement that doesn't reflect that is a bad arrangement.

Epilogue

The Future in Advertising: Where Do We Go from Here?

The future of advertising—where's it going? The crystal ball is indeed a dangerous instrument, but let's live dangerously and speculate on what advertising might be like beyond the year 2000 . . .

1 *Clutter* will be around for awhile, but we'll see some creative solutions. Enough among us will realize that the public has its saturation point—it will not sit still for its favorite programs being interrupted every ten minutes for three-and-a-half minutes of loud, smug, self-indulgent exercises by advertisers. Both cable and network TV will likely experiment with running ads at the beginning and end of an uninterrupted program, calling five minutes or so of commercials some umbrella name like *Viewers Gallery of Values*—a kind of "mini-Home Shopping Network."

2 *Real products* will be plugged more by name within the program. Instead of offering a cup of coffee, it will be

"How about a cup of Maxwell House?" or "We'll be fly-ing Pan Am to London tomorrow." Rising production costs and reduced budgets will necessitate producers finding new revenue sources such as this—or more so.

3   In something of a quasi-reversal of the preceding point, *advertisers will sue* news shows for contending that certain types of coverage mislead the public while con-sciously presenting the advertisers in an unfavorable light. Such statements as "In the third crash of a ———— airlines jet this season . . ." make people nervous about flying the line. The program certainly would never con-sider saying 113 airlines got from one place to another without incident today. Of course an air disaster is news, but the reporting is often totally irresponsible.

4   *Cable* will continue to fine-tune itself with specialty channels. We already have *MTV* (Music Television), *FNN* (Financial News Network), *ESPN* (Entertainment, Sports & News), *TNN* (Country Music and lifestyle from Nash-ville) and other channels for religion, weather, nostalgia and foreign language programming. With media costs soaring, budgets shrinking and so much more from which to choose, the advertiser who traditionally opted straight for the network will find value in moving media budgets to the specialty channel that best targets a pros-pect. Ditto with magazines—more will be introduced or clearly aimed at market segments (*Florida Life, Fifty Plus, Sh-Boom, Lears, Entrepreneur Woman* and *PC*, for example).

5   *Advertising* will, in the best traditions of the "new and improved" products, *repackage its services* to clients. Just as junk mail evolved into "direct marketing," con-tests and sweepstakes into "sales promotions" and phone soliciting "telemarketing," we will likely take the cue from the trade association, the American Association of Advertising Agencies, and present to clients not merely *advertising*, but *integrated communications*. This generally implies that the research and public relations divisions will get better billing in the presentation meeting.

6   The next round of *mergers* in advertising will be among smaller agencies, who will say they are consolidating to present clients with greater depth and strength to compete with the largest agencies . . . from which the owners of the small agencies were fired during the mega-merger cycle of the 1980s.

7   *Merchandising* will be a much bigger part of advertising as agencies become better negotiators for trades as well as "value added" promotions. That is to say, the media will pay for a number of the shirts, pens, baseball caps and other items bearing the advertisers name.

8   *Research* will be harder to sell. Here's why: things are cyclical. The generation of MBA baby boomers leading marketing departments tend to rely heavily on research to make a decision. By 2000, if they are still alive, the boomers will be in their mid-fifties and will want to sell (as agencies used to) their experience and expertise. *They* know how to sell product. They will have by then been at it for twenty or so years and that will be worth some clout in the presentation, most likely at the expense of research.

9   The *traditional thirty-second TV commercial* will be nearly extinct. Again, rising costs, shrinking budgets and a larger field of available media will offer more unique opportunities from split "30s" (two fifteen-second spots for separate products from the same company) or "90s," which in the best old classroom example will tell the audience what they are about to see advertised, advertise it and then tell them what they just saw.

10   The advertising industry will create an award honoring the best award presented for advertising.

The Crash Course in Advertising

Good advertising grows from smart marketing, strategic planning, and good creative talent. Good advertising is simply very good communication—with a point. Several points, actually. They are:

- Hype is not good advertising.
- We should not manipulate consumer expectations for our products to a level the product cannot possibly satisfy.
- Lying about products is not good advertising. Overstating the case may sometimes be entertaining but . . . has anyone actually ever *seen* a person grinning and screaming over the incredible-bombastic-savings-valuathon at the automobile dealers showroom? Most people, if ever greeted by such wild-eyed salesmen shouting "We're dealin' now," would flee in fear.
- People do smile and say things like "Hey, that's really *good*," when something looks or tastes or sounds or feels good to them.

- People do not make a sound like "Boing!" or burst into song and re-evaluate the quality of life because glassware sparkles or clothing comes out clean after washing. They *expected* it to come out clean.
- Are clients jerks? No.
- Are ad people superficial, shallow, unethical incompetents?
- Mostly no.
- Believing the adage "everything works if you let it," here are some do's and don'ts for good advertising campaigns:

Don't do this:

1   Don't create ad messages the CEO wants to hear; create ad messages the *customer* wants to hear.

2   Don't make outrageous claims that insult the intelligence of your audience.

3   Don't make ads for your portfolio, your relatives or for awards; make ads for your customers.

4   Don't do "something like what that other guy did."

5   Don't insist that because you bought the whole space, you've go to *fill* the whole space with unnecessary, self-serving or irrelevant words or pictures.

6   Don't be big and loud just to be big and loud. It may get attention, but it also annoys.

7   Don't make ads that are stupid, smirk or suggest arrogance.

8   Don't let your ad ever qualify to be called "clutter."

Do this:

1   Identify your audience with thorough research.

2   Test, qualify, quantify.

3   Be honest. Remember your public has a long memory about products and companies that deceive them.

4   Be believable. Hype has a very short success period.

5   Be positive. If the best you can say about your product is that your *competitor's* isn't very good, you're in big trouble with your product.

6   Trust your instincts.

7   Go against trends.

8   Take risks.

9   Talk about benefits, a promise, a reason to buy.

10   Be distinctive. Put personality into the brand and its ads.

11   Stand for something. Let your customer know what you've got and why they should want it.

12   Keep it simple. Customers want to know what's in it for them. Tell them.

13   Expect to succeed.

14   Frequency is important, but the quality of your message is *more* important.

15   Tell the media rep who says you'll be conspicuous by your absence from the special issue that the whole point of advertising is to be conspicuous. And different.

16   Know what things cost. It is one thing to expect your agency to work hard for you and make great deals. It's something else to expect too much.

17   Demand that your agency have good negotiating skills. Remnants (heavily discounted media opportunities), frequency discounts, bonus ads and merchandising are all added value options available. Your agency should know them and use them to your advantage.

Sources and Resources

One of the more painful phrases an executive can utter is, "I didn't know that." None of us is expected to know everything, but persons responsible for advertising should know what's going on in the advertising business. Not the minutiae of industry staff promotions and second market agency billings, but those matters that can have a significant impact on advertising or the communications industry as a whole.

For example, when cigarette ads were banned from radio and television, you didn't have to be the head of a tobacco company to consider the effect such a move could have on a wide range of concerns from ad rates to broadcast standards. Consider the acceptability of feminine hygiene product and condom ads, underwear advertising and public service announcements for medical, social and environmental issues. These significantly altered the temperature of the marketplace. Things too controversial or personal to even mention just a few years ago are now common. It is more than useful, it is *critical* for communications executives to be aware of the market envi-

219

ronment if there is truly a desire to maximize a campaign's effectiveness and cost efficiencies. The direction a competitor charts in advertising and marketing can change the course of an industry.

Not only is knowledge power, it is easier to acquire than ever before. Most major cities' newspapers devote increasingly more space to marketing news. *The Wall Street Journal*, in redefining its layout in three sections, devotes a major portion of section two to advertising and marketing. Typically such subjects as telemarketing, direct mail, cable TV and broadcasting changes brought about by innovation or regulation are the focus.

Less than a decade ago many observers were predicting the demise or dramatic reduction in the number of magazines and newspapers. In fact the very opposite has occurred. More to the point, *Time, Newsweek, U.S. News* and *World Report* and even *People* magazine now frequently chronicle the executive suite activities of the TV networks, film studios and each other in a manner formerly reserved for politicians and movies stars. Ted Turner, Rupert Murdoch, Donald Trump, Michael Eisner, Laurence Tish and Brandon Tartikoff, to name a few, have become cover stories in magazines and guests on talk shows. And the news these people make will usually influence where and how products will be marketed . . . and for how much.

In addition to a good daily dose of general news, as in every other profession, those who go the extra mile will benefit from the effort. Here is a brief summary of some of advertising material by the column and by the volume. Company ad people should know what's happening in the communications industry. Start here.

Trade Publications

Advertising Age, published weekly by Crain Communications, 740 N. Rush, Chicago, IL 60611, has been regarded as the "bible" of the ad industry since it began publishing. While a preeminent trade publication, *Ad Age* is an easy read, both informational and entertaining to industry people and nonprofessionals alike. Major industry news is presented with front-page banner headlines and all the flair of a daily paper. Inside is an interesting mix of both late-breaking news and lengthy, well-developed pieces, features, editorials, critiques of new campaigns and many reader letters and guest editorials. The paper thrives on airing all sides of controversies. James Brady offers two columns per issue, one a gossipy roundup of personality notes and industry tidbits, the other an essay that more often than not has little to do with the business but is always quotable, thought-provoking and usually very funny. *Ad Age* is a showcase for an industry that likes to talk about itself, for better or for worse.

Adweek is published sixty-one times per year (basically weekly with several additional special editions on specialized subjects such as cable television, sales promotion and so on.) by A/S/M Communications, 435 N. Michigan, Chicago, IL 60611, or 49 E. 21st Street, New York, NY 10010. If *Ad Age* is the bible, *Adweek* would like you to change religions. A highly aggressive magazine, it covers hot industry news trends and offers a group of insightful columnists. Writing is tight and each issue is weighty with information.

Television/Radio Age, is published alternate Mondays by Television Editorial Corporation, 1270 Avenue of the Americas, New York, NY 10020. While the two previously noted trade publications are very good, they occasionally blur the line between newspaper and magazine, news and feature. This one's a magazine and it's news. Agency media and account professionals who focus on TV and radio read this publication carefully for "roundtable" articles in which media execs sound off on subjects from cable to spot sales to regulation to programming strategies. This is not a casual or general interest publication, but very specialized, with considerable space devoted to industry personnel shifts and what the presence of these individuals may mean in their new posts.

Marketing & Media Decisions is published monthly by Decisions Publications, 401 Park Avenue South, New York, NY 10016. This is a very slick, very departmentalized magazine, heavy on graphics and features. Typically, each issue has something for everybody—a book review, research article, outdoor story, yellow pages. Overall there's a fair overview of "marketing & media" information, with no apparent attempt to cover late news or to "scoop" the competition, as is often the case with trade publications.

Inside Media (formerly *Inside Print*) is published twenty-four times a year by Hanson Publishing Group, Six River Bend, Box 4272, Stamford, CT 06907-0949. An extremely well-designed, well-written magazine that provided good information for those with budgets largely concentrated in magazine and newspaper advertising changed its format to look more like *Ad Age*. It's slick and colorful. A typical issue might focus articles on consultants ("The Media Doctors Are In") or merchandising ("Buying the Sizzle"). Departments are clean and specific on magazines, television and newspapers. As trade publications go, rate this one interesting, useful, but nonessential to keeping up with the business.

Electronic Media is published weekly by Crain Communications, 740 N. Rush, Chicago, IL 60611. This broadcast publication uses a newspaper style to report on mergers and acquisitions, cable and broadcast trends, deals and forecasts. It is useful to the extent that it takes the public pulse of what's working and what isn't in electronic media—no minor considerations to advertisers.

Broadcasting is published weekly by Broadcasting Publications, 1705 DeSales Street, N.W., Washington, DC 20036. This magazine covers radio, television, cable and satellite communications and largely focuses on changes in FCC rules, ratings and dealmaking. Again, if electronic media is a significant portion of the ad budget, keeping track of that industry' shifts and trends is important.

The Information Catalog is published by FIND/SVP, 625 Avenue of the Americas, New York, NY 10011. This catalog offers a compendia of reports, studies, surveys and reference books in some forty industries, focusing on such areas as market share, technological advances and competitive positioning. It is clearly a reference publication, not designed for casual reading.

American Demographics is published monthly by American Demographics, Inc., 108 North Cayuga Street, Ithaca, NY 14850. It calls itself "The Magazine of Consumer Markets" and is a publication of Dow Jones, which, as publisher of *The Wall Street Journal* and other international news vehicles, offers instant authority and credibility. The magazine is on heavy, high-quality paper stock and has the look and feel of a publication that wants to be taken seriously. It should be, as both a research magazine and a business book. Typical articles: "How to Select a Market Research Firm" and "Inside America's Households." Plenty of charts, graphs and statistics should please the numbers lovers. Its supplement, *Marketing Tools Alert*, offers a very useful mix of charts and statistics, but is primarily a catalog of first-class books and tapes on Demographics, Marketing, Marketing Research and a wide, yet related, range of subjects.

Books

Advertising and marketing is not just gray flannel suits, Madison Avenue and alphabet corporate names. As mainstream America takes more of an interest in the subject, the quality of material on it becomes both more focused and more plentiful, from memoirs to "how-to" books. Here are some of the best, all of which should be available in local book stores or can be special-ordered:

Ogilvy on Advertising by David Ogilvy, Crown Publishers, Inc., 1983. Also available in paperback from Vintage Press.

The Trouble with Advertising—A View from the Inside by John O'Toole, Chelsea House Publishers, 1980. Also in paperback from Times Books.

Marketing Immunity: Breaking through Customer Resistance by George Lazarus with Bruce Wexler, Dow Jones Irwin Books, 1988.

Future Scope—Success Strategies for the 1990's & Beyond by Joe Cappo, Longman Financial Services Publishing, 1989.

Radio Advertising by Bob Schulberg, NTC Business Books, 1989.

The Ad Game—Playing to Win by G. Robert Cox and Edward J. McGee, Prentice-Hall, Inc., 1990.

Confessions of an Advertising Man by David Ogilvy, Atheneum Macmillan Publishing Co., 1963, 1987. Available in paperback.

For a change of pace, consider this useful, but not exactly light reading:

Standard Directory of Advertising Agencies (The Agency Red Book), published by National Register Publishing Company, 3004 Glenview Rd., Wilmette, IL 60091. Phone 708-441-2210.

Standard Rate & Data Service (SRDS) sold separately, these are the essential directories of media information:

1. Business Publication Rates and Data
2. Newspaper Rates and Data
3. Newspaper Circulation Analysis
4. Consumer Magazine and Agri-Media Rates and Data
5. Spot Television Rates and Data
6. Spot Radio Rates and Data
7. Spot Radio—Small Markets Edition

8. Direct Mail List Rates and Data
9. Print Media Production Data
10. Special Issues (Business Publications, Consumer Magazines, Newspapers)
11. Card Deck Rates and Data
12. Hispanic Media and Markets
13. Community Publication Rates and Data
14. Canadian Advertising Rates and Data
15. Lifestyle Market Analyst

For detailed information or subscriptions, write or call SRDS, 3004 Glenview Rd., Wilmette, IL 60091. Phone 708-256-8333 or 1-800-323-4588.

Glossary: Coming to Terms With Terms

In a meeting of client and agency people, many terms are circulated: GRPs, CPMs, ADI. The assumption is that everyone knows what everyone else is talking about, or should know. Actually, everyone *doesn't* always know and rarely will anyone ask. In an effort to both prevent embarrassment and raise the level of such meetings, we offer a simple list of the words and terms most frequently used in advertising.

This is not intended to replace the office dictionary. It also doesn't offer definitions of words such as *advertising, marketing* or *media*. If you don't have a sense of those by this time, these won't help.

ABC: (1) In network radio and television, the common reference for the American Broadcasting Company. (2) In newspaper and magazine publishing, the Audit Bureau of Circulations which issues statements verifying circulation figures claimed by the publications.

ADI: The area of dominant influence, a geographic designation by Arbitron Ratings Company of broadcast stations having the greater share of audience/households as distinguished from other areas.

AIDA: A four-step theory that presumes to identify necessary elements of effective advertising: attention, interest, desire, action.

AIO: A term used in research as to the determination of activities, interests, opinions.

Audimeter: A.C. Nielsen Company's electronic device which monitors when, at which channel, and for the length of time a television set is on.

Barter: Simply stated, trading. In advertising, a product is provided with a provision to receive other products or services in return. Typically in a television show barter a program is offered to a local station with a certain number of advertisements included, with the local station permitted to sell available commercial spots to other advertisers; trading ads for products.

Below-the-line: Non-media marketing, typically advertising expenses outside of the ad budget (such as sales promotion).

Bookends: In media, the practice of buying two fifteen-second commercials to run before and after a longer spot.

Borrowed interest: Using an unrelated subject to attract attention to an ad message.

Brand name: The trademarked or service marked true name of a product or service.

Brand retailing: A term used increasingly as synonymous with sales promotion.

Call-to action: The element of an ad that directs the audience to take action immediately and presents an address or phone number.

CBS: In network radio and television, the Columbia Broadcasting System.

Closing date: The last date on which media will accept ads for a specified issue or program. The "closing date for material" is the date shortly after the closing date when commercial material must be received by the media to which the commitment has been made.

Clutter: An imbalance of advertising over other subject matter, causing the ad's message to be lost or indistinguishable.

Commission system: In advertising, a method of compensation by which an agency receives a commission (typically 15 percent) from the media for advertising purchased for a particular client.

Comp: A composite rendering for presentation, showing a facsimile of elements assembled to closely reflect how a finished ad will look (photos, typeset copy, illustration, etc.).

CNN: Acronym for cable television's Cable News Network.

CPM (cost per thousand): The cost of an ad divided by the circulation of the publication or audience size (viewership or listenership) and multiplied by 1,000; the standard method of reasonably determining the value of a form of advertising by determining what it costs to deliver the ad message to 1,000 persons.

CPR (cost per rating): The cost of a commercial ad spot divided by the rating of the particular media on which it appears, as typically determined by Nielsen or Arbitron.

DAR (day-after-recall): In research, a test to determine the extent to which persons can recall an ad's characteristics one day after exposure to it.

Demographics: In research, the characteristic breakdown of a particular (targeted) audience, according to such criteria as age, gender, income, geographical location, marital status.

DMA (designated market area): Much the way Arbitron Company establishes an Area of Dominant Influence

(ADI), this is the Nielsen Company's measure of the greater share of the television viewing audience in one geographic area over another.

Fee system: A standard ad agency compensation system by which the agency is paid by the client for all services rendered, as opposed to being compensated by commissions from media or other purchases.

FNN: Acronym for the Financial News Network, a cable television network primarily programming business news.

Focus group: A research method by which a small group of persons is assembled according to particular qalifications and interviewed on a subject as a group rather than individually.

GRP (Gross Rating Point): In media, the sum of the rating points for a particular program or time period to determine the size of the audience.

Hook: Whether a headline, music, picture or sound, the central attention-getting feature of an ad.

House ad: Media's use of unsold time or space to advertise its own publications, services, programs or company.

Image ads: Advertising created to influence consumer perception of the product or service in a way that may or may not approximate reality; usually emotionally oriented, as opposed to *corporate* (also called *institutional*) ads, which emphasize the advertiser's name and presence more than attempting to influence how the public feels about the product; or *retail* advertising, which aggressively emphasizes the sales message and the "call to action."

Institutional market: In general advertising this term refers to schools, hospitals, churches and museums and such, as opposed to members of the general public as individuals. In financial marketing the term applies to pension funds, trust accounts and so on, again as opposed to individuals.

Keyline: The assembled components of a print ad ready for reproduction.

Layout: The general outline or plan for a print ad indicating where its component parts (such as headline, photo, copy) appear.

Makegood: A free ad offered to an advertiser when a scheduled ad failed to run as agreed or was somehow otherwise mishandled in such a way as to disadvantage the advertiser.

Mature market: Term used to describe older target market group, usually over sixty-five years of age; seniors market; not necessarily retired persons.

Media mix: The strategic plan and budget allocation for targeting a specific group with a combination of media such as newspapers, magazines, outdoor ads, local or network TV and/or radio, etc.

Mechanicals (or mechanical art): A representation of a print ad in its final or near-final form.

MSO (Multiple System Operator): A company owning and operating more than a single cable television system.

NBC: In network television, the National Broadcasting Company, a unit of the General Electric Corp.

Needle drop: Using pre-recorded, commercially available or stock catalog music or effects in a television or radio spot, as opposed to using music or sound effects originally written or recorded for the spot.

Point of purchase (POP) or *point of sale ad:* Advertising at the actual location where the product or service is offered for sale, such as a supermarket or other store display, poster in travel agency, office, etc.

Positioning: Placement or comparison of the product or service in relation to its competition or a larger universe.

Rate card: In media, the printed list of costs and conditions for the purchase of print space or broadcast time.

Recall tests: In market research, a form of test in which the interview subject is asked to recall information presented in an ad some time after having viewed or heard the ad.

Remnant: Unsold media time or space after the closing date for the acceptance of ads, made available at a heavily discounted rate.

Retail advertising: Ads offering products or services with a sense of immediacy, such as sales or discounts to consumers, as distinguished from image or corporate advertising.

Seniors market: Older audience—see "Mature market."

Snipe: A small but bold element or addition to a printed piece or ad used to call special attention to a feature of the subject, such as "new improved," "last days," "held over," "sold out," etc.

Spot sales: In radio or television advertising, the advertiser may purchase commercial time on a selected market basis, rather than buying time on the entire network or cable system.

Storyboard: In television advertising a sequence of visuals drawn to show the action and dialogue of a proposed commercial prior to its production.

Subliminal advertising: A theory that suggests that an ad can carry messages that cannot be noticed on a conscious level.

UPC (Universal Price Code or Universal Product Code): System of marking merchandise with a series of bars or lines so that a scanner may provide information to a computer for budget, sales, inventory and other controls.

Upfront: The practice of selling advertising well in advance of the media presentation date, such as selling commercial air time on network television's fall schedule shows during the preceding summer, before shows have been introduced to viewers.

USP (unique selling propositions): That element of the advertised message that offers the qualities or characteristics which differentiate the advertised product or service from its competition.

Value added: In advertising, this term has become synonymous with merchandising, adding additional bonus elements to enhance a sale, such as a publication offering a free page of advertising for every certain number of pages purchased or a bonus in television or radio spot time or event tickets, etc.

Voiceover: The narration or "voice" of the unseen spokesperson in a broadcast ad.

WOM: Term sometimes used to identify word-of-mouth advertising.

Bibliography and References

Advertising Age: "Ad Spending By 100 Leaders (1988),"
published September 27, 1989; "Carnation Links pay,
Research" by Nancy Magiera, March 6, 1989; "The
Three Most Important Questions in Advertising" by
Hank Seiden, May 22, 1989; "What the '90s Will
Hold for Focus Group Research" by Thomas L.
Greenbaum, January 22, 1990; "The Party's Over" by
Julie Liesse Erickson and Judann Dagnoli, February
27, 1989.

Advertising & Marketing Checklists by Ron Kaatz, NTC
Books, 1989.

Advertising Theory and Practice by C. H. Sandage and Vernon Fryburger, Richard D. Irwin, Inc., 1963.

Advertising—What It Is and How to Do It by Roderick
White, McGraw-Hill Book Company (UK) Limited,
1980 and 1988.

Adweek: Tip O'Neill's ad deals, November 6, 1989; "10
Reasons To Think Small" by Tony Benjamin, July 31,
1989; "Festering Crisis of Conscience Surfaces in

'How to Get Ahead in Advertising'" by Jane Weaver, May 15, 1989; "The New Reality: Now that Advertising's Hit Bottom, There's Nowhere to Go But Up" by Richard Morgan, May 19, 1990; "Terminal Insecurity: Why Agencies Don't Put Integrity Over Money" by Richard Morgan, October 2, 1989; "Choosing an Agency" December 1, 1986.

All I Really Need to Know, I Learned in Kindergarten by Robert Fulgham, Villard Books, 1989.

American Demographics statistical data on newspapers, television, radio and magazines, October, 1989.

Beware the Naked Man Who Offers You His Shirt by Harvey Mackay, William Morrow & Company, 1990.

Business Month "The Great Debate" September, 1989.

Confessions of an Advertising Man by David Ogilvy, Atheneum/Macmillan Publishing Co., 1963, 1988.

Choosing an Advertising Agency by William M. Weilbacher, Crain Books/NTC, 1983.

Dictionary of Marketing Terms by Peter D. Bennett, American Marketing Association, 1988.

Essentials of Advertising Strategy by Don E. Schultz and Stanley I. Tannenbaum, NTC Business Books, 1988.

Future Scope by Joe Cappo, Longman Financial Services Publishing, 1989.

Manhattan, inc. "The Bare Facts About Marty Weiss" by Rachel Abramowitz, January, 1989; "Fred and Alan Love Lucy" by Judith Newman, February, 1990.

Marketing & Media Decisions: "Ethics: A Pragmatic View" by Allan V. Palmer, July, 1988; "Mediology" by Ed Papagian, February, 1989.

The Mature Market: A Strategic Marketing Guide to America's Fastest Growing Population Segment" by Robert Menchin, Probus, 1989.

Ogilvy on Advertising by David Ogilvy, Crown Publishers, 1983.

People Skills by Robert Bolton, Simon & Schuster, 1979.

Radio Advertising by Bob Schulberg, NTC Books, 1989.

Standard Directory of Advertising Agencies (The Agency Redbook), National Register Publishing Company.

Strategy in Advertising by Les Bogart, NTC Business Books, 1984, 1986.

The Ad Game, —Playing to Win— by G. Robert Cox and Edward J. McGee, Prentice-Hall, Inc., 1990.

Subliminal Seduction by Wilson Brian Key, Prentice Hall, 1973.

Trouble with Advertising, The by John O'Toole, Chelsea House Publishers, 1980.

Up the Organization by Robert Townsend, Alfred A. Knopf, Inc., 1970.

U.S. News & World Report: Michael Jackson, LA Gear and Pepsi deals, September 25, 1989; "Science 1, Advertisers O" May 1, 1989.

Wall Street Journal, The Paul McCartney/Visa story; "Research Gains Followers, Agencies Point Out Its Failures" by Joanne Lipman, April 5, 1989.

Index

U.S. Marines, 125
United States Savings Bonds, 143
UPC (Universal Price Code), 232
Upfront, 232
US Borax, 153

V
V-8 Vegetable Juice, 125
Value added, 189, 233
Van Kampen Merritt, 87, 133, 134, 161-63
Video cassettes, 185
Virginia Slims Cigarettes, 125
Visa, 153
Voiceover, 233
Volkswagen, 140, 152

W
Wal-Mart, 165
Washington National Insurance Company, 135
Wayne, John, 144, 154
Weber Cohn & Riley, 41
Weight Watchers, 153
Weilbacher, William M., 36, 38, 47
Weiss, Marty, 116
Wendy's, 125, 140, 161, 164
Westinghouse, 125
Wheaties, 125
White, Roderick, 63
Willis, Bruce, 154
Wine coolers, 154
Winston Cigarettes, 125
Winwood, Steve, 154
Wisk Detergent, 125
WOM (word of mouth) advertising, 233
Wonder, Stevie, 154
Wonder Bread, 125
WPP Group, 63, 66
Wrigley's Double Mint Gum, 125

Y
York Furrier, 129

Z
Zenith, 125